'I have read these commentaries with great joy. They are all that one could hope for – accessible, clear, exegetically reliable and devotionally warm-hearted. We need more like this! This book is a gem – buy it and read it. It will do you great good.'

The Rt. Revd. Wallace Benn
Bishop of Lewes

Focus on the Bible Commentaries

Genesis – John Currid*
Exodus – John L. Mackay*
Deuteronomy – Alan Harman*
Judges and Ruth – Stephen Dray
1 and 2 Samuel – David Searle*
1 and 2 Kings – Robert Fyall*
Proverbs – Eric Lane (1999)
Jeremiah – George Martin*
Ezekiel – Anthony Billington*
Daniel – Robert Fyall
Hosea – Michael Eaton
Amos – O Palmer Robertson*
Jonah-Zephaniah – John L. Mackay
Haggai-Malachi – John L. Mackay
Matthew – Charles Price
Mark – Geoffrey Grogan
John – Robert Peterson (2001)
Romans – R. C. Sproul
2 Corinthians – Geoffrey Grogan
Galatians – Joseph Pipa*
Ephesians – R. C. Sproul
Philippians – Hywel Jones
1 and 2 Thessalonians – Richard Mayhue (1999)
The Pastoral Epistles – Douglas Milne
Hebrews – Walter Riggans
James – Derek Prime
1 Peter – Derek Cleave
2 Peter/Jude – Paul Gardner
Revelation – Steve Motyer*

Journey Through the Old Testament – Bill Cotton
How To Interpret the Bible – Richard Mayhue

Those marked with an * are currently being written.

2 Peter
and
Jude

Paul Gardner

Christian Focus

Rev. Dr. Paul Gardner is a minister and Rural Dean in the Church of England. He and his wife Sharon, a teacher, now live in Hartford, Cheshire, and have three children, Jonathan, David and Hannah. Formerly Dr. Gardner was a lecturer in New Testament at Oak Hill Theological College in London.

© Paul Gardner
ISBN 1 85792 338 3

Published in 1998
by
Christian Focus Publications,
Geanies House, Fearn, Ross-shire,
IV20 1TW, Great Britain.

2 PETER

JUDE

2
Peter

Introduction

This short New Testament letter from the apostle Peter deals with a number of very important subjects that remain as significant for the church and the individual Christian today as they were in the first century. In spite of his concern that the people to whom he is writing should be on their guard against false teaching, Peter's letter delights in such major themes as the awesome sovereignty of God, the glorious return of Jesus Christ; the full trustworthiness of God's Word in Scripture; and the sheer joy and excitement of growing in the knowledge of God and living for him.

Relationship to Jude

Anyone asked to write a commentary on 2 Peter is invariably also asked to write a commentary on the epistle of Jude. At first glance this may seem strange. Why shouldn't commentaries on 1 Peter and 2 Peter be bound together? Why Jude and 2 Peter? The answer to this is not easy but is best explained by comparing 2 Peter chapter 2 with Jude. The similarities between them are obvious even on a superficial reading. This relationship has been explained in a variety of ways. Generally it falls into three categories: a) 2 Peter borrowed from Jude; b) Jude borrowed from 2 Peter; c) both Jude and 2 Peter used a similar or the same source material. Jude is only twenty-five verses long and fifteen of these appear in at least a very similar form in 2 Peter 2. It is impossible to be absolutely certain who actually wrote first.

However, it should be noted that even if Peter borrowed, in this case from Jude, there is still no need to exclude apostolic authorship of 2 Peter, as some have suggested. They argue that a great apostle would not draw on a minor figure like Jude. Such a suggestion, though, fails adequately to take account of two facts. Firstly, Jude was also regarded as having apostolic authority and secondly, as many have pointed out, literature is full of examples of great writers who have borrowed from those less well known than themselves.

The reasons some say Jude drew on 2 Peter can seem plausible enough but problems arise for both the view that Peter borrowed from Jude and vice versa. For example, it is said that:

a) Peter often talks about the false teachers in the future tense, while Jude already views them as present. Some even suggest that Jude 17-18 looks back to 2 Peter 3:2, 3. Yet, it must be added that Peter does not always use the future tense of these heretics (e.g. 2 Peter 2:10, 13; 3:16).

b) Jude is more polished in its structure than is 2 Peter, and this may indicate a careful and reflective re-working of Peter's material. However, it may also mean that Peter simply remembered Jude's work and re-wrote it in a more relaxed way.

c) It is also often asked why Jude should have bothered to re-write 2 Peter in such a very short letter, while adding a minimum of his own ideas. However, Jude himself tells us that he writes with a certain urgency (Jude 3) and 'to remind you'. So perhaps he found Peter's letter to be the most useful message to pass on (again?) to the congregation.

My own view is that probably Jude and 2 Peter were written around the same time, but I am unpersuaded by any of the arguments supporting either those who believe Jude was written first or those who believe 2 Peter was written first.

One thing I certainly believe is this: the arguments about who came first and who borrowed from whom and the similarities of the epistles have clouded much of the teaching we find in both epistles. Similarities there are, and this may suggest that some of the false teaching in both churches was similar, but the differences are considerable as well. 2 Peter has much more in it that is not found in Jude than is. It tackles some different themes and so we must never be tempted to assume that if we have studied the one book we can virtually ignore the other. More is said on this when we look at 2 Peter 2:4 below.

Peter as author

Many argue that Peter, the apostle, did not write this letter. I believe he did for two reasons. The evidence against Petrine authorship is unconvincing and often depends upon building one hypothesis upon another when each hypothesis is surprisingly weak. The main reasons given against Peter's authorship are usually that:

a) the language is too 'Hellenised' for a Jewish fisherman to have written;

b) 1 Peter and 2 Peter are too different in style and content to be by the same author;

c) the letter would appear to have been written later than the mid sixties AD when Peter was put to death under Nero. One reason given for this is that it refers to Paul's letters as Scripture (3:16).

Another reason for not regarding this as truly from Peter looks to the so-called 'genre' of the letter which is regarded as a 'testament'. Nevertheless, none of these arguments is particularly persuasive.

Peter had worked among Greek-speaking Gentiles for many years and was no doubt able to adopt a suitable writing style for his audience just as any capable writer these days can do. The difference between the styles of 1 and 2 Peter can be accounted for by the fact that Silvanus (Silas) acted as a 'secretary' in the first epistle (1 Peter 5:12). Also it is worth noting that while 2 Peter may have been written to the same group of churches as 1 Peter (2 Peter 3:1 suggests this might be the case), it is by no means certain. 2 Peter 3:1 might well be a reference to a letter of which we have no record.

Above we noted that the 'genre' of the letter is sometimes regarded as a 'testament', i.e. as in a 'last will and testament'. Some existing documents like this were written by others after the person's death, and so it is suggested was 2 Peter. But it seems to me that if we take this letter at face value, then Peter is indeed writing something of a 'testament', but he is writing it himself from Rome knowing that his death is imminent. Other literary 'testaments' are not easily compared with 2 Peter because they are not usually in a 'letter' form.

The second main reason for accepting Petrine authorship relates to a doctrine of Scripture. Normally it is good to take Scripture at face value unless there are clear indications in the text itself that this should not be done. The claims of this epistle to be by Peter and written towards the end of his life make sense and are thoroughly believable.

The traditional view that the epistle was written from Rome to a group of churches with which both Paul and Peter had had contact seems to fit the evidence. Given the 'testament' themes running through the letter, it is natural to assume, as most have traditionally assumed, that it was written in the early to mid sixties just before Peter was put to death in the persecutions of Christians under Nero.

Relevance for Today

Peter was writing to a church or churches paralleled by many today – where false teaching was on the rise. He warned against the false teachings that denied the return of Christ, and allowed a weakening in moral conduct. His concern is that the original message of the gospel and the promise of Christ's return should not be forgotten. That 'core' gospel is centred in historical facts which include eye-witness testimony from the apostles, and in the truth of revealed Scripture.

Some of the more radical elements of today's church often sit light to history, repudiate the utter trustworthiness of Scripture, and look to apostolic testimony as religious 'myth'. Even the Second Coming is regarded as a 'myth' or, at best, some form of 'universalism' is often taught in which the possibility of a final judgment for the ungodly is denied. The teaching of this epistle offers a strong challenge to such radical theology. Yet it also challenges the more theologically conservative church, with a reminder of the sudden return of the Lord, and the need for lives that are godly and reflect the fruit of the Spirit. It challenges all Christians to maintain a godly perspective on this life – for we live in a period of grace – and to grow in grace and in the knowledge of the Lord so as to remain on guard against those who would lead believers astray.

A largely Gentile audience

Unlike the epistle of Jude which was probably written to a predominantly converted Jewish congregation, it would seem that Peter was writing to a church of mainly Gentile believers. When he talks of 'a faith as precious as ours', Peter is probably comparing the Gentile converts with those like Peter himself who have a Jewish background. We cannot be sure which church or group of churches Peter was writing to, but if they are the same as 1 Peter, and he does call this his 'second letter to them' (3:1), then they would have lived in what is now modern Turkey, and the churches would have been made up largely of Gentile converts.

Chapter 2 is full of allusions not just to the Old Testament but also to some intertestamental Jewish literature and some have suggested this indicates a church of predominantly Jewish background. However, we know from much of the New Testament that converts of all nationalities were quickly taught the Old Testament. Also, unlike Jude, Peter does not actually mention the Book of Enoch even though drawing upon it. This may also suggest that, whereas it was known by Jude's more Jewish audience, it was not known by Peter's audience. Additionally the Greek that is used in this epistle is fairly sophisticated suggesting perhaps that Peter was writing for Gentiles and adapting the gospel message to their language and world of ideas.

Overview of the letter

Peter begins in chapter 1 with the basic message of which he wishes to remind the congregation. The purpose of this reminder is given in verses 10-11. As Peter nears the end of his life he wishes, again, to insist on the absolute truth of what has been proclaimed, thus combating those who argued the message was based on 'cleverly invented stories' (verse 16). He urges his readers to recognise that spiritual life is about continuing growth in the knowledge of the Lord, a growth in understanding that leads to action.

In the second chapter Peter takes time to draw attention to the rise of false teachers, arguing that the Old Testament has made it clear that such people will be judged on the Last Day. These teachers have 'secretly' introduced 'destructive heresies, even denying the sovereign Lord' (verse 1).

Chapter three draws attention to the effect that 'scoffers' and others will have among these Christians, but God's Word and his promises are utterly to be trusted. Christ will return and that should be an encouragement to his people. Meanwhile, they should live holy lives (verse 11) and grow in the grace and knowledge of Jesus Christ (verse 18) for there is work to be done!

An Outline of the Epistle and Commentary

1.   **Greetings from Simon Peter (1:1-2)**

2.   **Peter's Gospel (1:3-11)**
   a)   The Gospel – Christ's provision (3)
   b)   The Gospel – Christ's great Promises (4)
   c)   The Gospel – the Christian Response (5-10).
           First, an effective and productive life
           Second, eagerness and effort
   d)   The Gospel – a rich welcome (11)

1. Greetings from Simon Peter (1:1-2)

Simon Peter, a servant and apostle of Jesus Christ, To those who through the righteousness of our God and Saviour Jesus Christ have received a faith as precious as ours (verse 1).

The first verse of this book reminds us that it was indeed written as a letter. It follows a standard form of opening which is found in several other New Testament letters. It indicates who wrote the letter and his role, then it briefly identifies the people who received the letter and their position as members of the Christian church. The greeting then follows in verse 2.

The author is the apostle Peter of whom we hear much in the Gospels and the book of Acts. In the Greek here we read **'Simeon** Peter, servant and apostle of Jesus Christ'. Simeon was a literal transliteration of the Hebrew name meaning 'hearing' – a name linked to Samuel ('God has heard'). Given that most people would have used the name 'Simon', the mention of 'Simeon' is another indication that Peter himself was the author, using his original Palestinian name.

Peter reminds his readers of his authority as he writes. He is **servant and apostle of Jesus Christ**. The word 'servant' is 'doulos' in Greek which can mean slave. The link of the word directly with the title 'apostle' reminds us of the opening of a number of Paul's letters (e.g. Rom. 1:1). Of course in one sense Peter is identifying with all Christians who wish to serve their Lord and Master after coming to faith. All Christians of that day and age would have known about slavery and many would have been slaves. The word would therefore have reminded them of the demands laid on them to serve Christ whole-heartedly and in every area of their life. However, for Peter, the two words together were probably a specific claim to apostolic authority.

In the Old Testament the title 'servant of the Lord' carried great significance because it had been specially applied to the 'greats' of the faith, people like Abraham, Moses and

David. Peter thus linked himself to the line of those who were called by God to have foundational ministries among his people. The word **apostle**[1] confirms this claim to authority. As we read in Ephesians 2:20: '... God's household, built on the foundation of the apostles and prophets'.

So Peter moves on to identify those to whom he is writing as **those who ... have received a faith as precious as ours**. He does not say where they live although they may be the same people as mentioned in 1 Peter, in which case they lived in modern day Turkey, places known as Pontus, Galatia, Cappadocia, Asia and Bithynia (1 Peter 1:1).

One of the great debates of the early church, in which Peter himself was often caught up, was whether Gentile Christians had the same status in the covenant community as Jewish Christians. It is important to remember that it was Peter himself who came back to the church leaders in Jerusalem in Acts 15:7-11 and argued that he had witnessed Gentiles receiving the same blessing and experiences as they had received on the Day of Pentecost. Gentiles had received the Holy Spirit as had believing Jews on the Day of Pentecost. Peter had argued that this was the clearest indication that both groups were now one in Christ. Neither group was superior to the other.

Even though Peter was an apostle and a Jew, these Gentile Christians had **a faith as precious as ours**. 'Faith' here is not the body of doctrine that we might find in a Creed, but

---

1. The word 'apostle' means 'messenger' and is the name given to the special twelve disciples chosen by Jesus. Later the apostle Paul was added to this special number. The fact that the apostles were eye-witnesses of Jesus gave their message a unique authority. They were God's choice (eg. Luke 6:12-13) and appointed by him as 'servants of the word' (Luke 1:2). In their ministries, therefore, they carried the authority to be speaking from and for God in the way the prophets had spoken in the Old Testament. Though many go out as messengers of the gospel even today, the ministry of these apostles was unique in its authority and foundational status.

refers to the believer's own commitment to the Lord Jesus.
This faith, this commitment to Jesus as God and Saviour, is
given him by God, hence Peter says they have 'received' it.
As with any specially valuable gift, the word precious is an
apt description.

In our day it is common to believe that faith is something
that we *do* in order to be saved. Peter knew otherwise. He
had lived through Pentecost and he had seen Gentiles caught
up in pagan darkness come to a living faith in the Lord Jesus
Christ and so he knew from experience that faith itself is a
gift of God. As Paul put it: 'faith comes from hearing and
hearing by the Word of Christ' (Rom. 10:17). What Peter
says here reminds us that we have no room to boast, but rather
we rejoice as Peter does at having received such a **precious**
gift that gives us status as members of the covenant
community. Whatever our background, nationality or race,
we belong to his people through believing faith.

Peter then speaks of the manner in which this faith has
been received: **through the righteousness of our God and
Saviour Jesus Christ**. This could refer to God's righteousness, meaning his fairness and justice in giving equal
status to all people of faith, whether Jew or Gentile.
Alternatively, it could refer to the righteousness by which
God puts people right with himself. This is the righteousness
he imputes[2] to his people as he ensures that they may be
declared 'not guilty' before the judgment seat of God. Either
is possible here, but the clear teaching that faith is 'received'
may well suggest that the latter understanding of righteousness
is correct here.

This righteousness is attributed to our God and Saviour
Jesus Christ. Among some scholars there is debate about
translating this phrase. Is this referring to both God and Jesus,

2. This word refers to the fact that God, as it were, 'credits' the righteousness
of Christ to our account.

('... God and our Saviour Jesus Christ', AV), or to Jesus as God, with the NIV? The latter is much more likely and well in line with the rest of this epistle (see for example, 1:11; 2:20; 3:2, 15, 18). Peter thus affirms the divinity of Christ.

This lengthy first verse identifies the authority with which Peter is writing, but also emphasises the precious gift of faith that his readers have received which is of equal standing with that of the apostles and Christians of a Jewish background. In line with people like Thomas (John 20:28), Peter quickly asserts the full divinity of Jesus as God who is the author of salvation.

In a modern world in which once again even Christian leaders are questioning the divinity of Jesus, it is good to remember that the apostles preached his divinity and wrote about it. It is as God that Jesus can be the righteous Saviour.

Grace and peace be yours in abundance (verse 2).
I have a friend who ends his letter 'grace and peace' followed by his signature. I rather like it. It is like a prayer for the person he is writing to, and this is how several New Testament letters begin. Peter is concerned that these people know and experience the continuing **grace** of God in their lives and the objective reality of **peace** with him **in abundance**. These are exactly the same words of greeting used by Peter in 1 Peter 1:2. These Christians have been saved and declared righteous and need to act in a way that enjoys and lives up to their new status as part of God's covenant people. Just as salvation itself is an undeserved gift from our God and Saviour Jesus Christ, so continuing in the covenant community of God's people must be entirely of grace. Peter is going to make much of this as the letter proceeds, so he prays that they will experience an **abundance** of that grace and continued peace with God.

Both **grace** and **peace** are words with a substantial background in the Old Testament. **Grace** points to the undeserved covenant love of the Lord so often experienced by the people of Israel (The Hebrew word *hesed* specially highlights this faithful covenant love of God for his people. It is often translated 'unfailing love' in the NIV). God's people have always known that it is not only entering the covenant relationship with God that is by grace but also remaining in that relationship with God. This is why his love is *unfailing*, and this ultimately is why we can have full assurance of our salvation. Peter will shortly re-affirm this assurance by drawing attention to the wonderful promises of God in verse 4.

Peace is another 'covenant' concept and reflects the Hebrew concept of *shalom*, the peace experienced by those who are God's people, who have been forgiven and who inherit his blessings. Isaiah 54:10 helps explain the way these two concepts come together in the covenant Lord's dealings with his people: ' "Though the mountains be shaken and the hills removed, yet my unfailing love for you will not be shaken nor my covenant of peace be removed," says the LORD, who has compassion on you.'

through the knowledge of God and of Jesus our Lord. Here Peter introduces a theme that also continues through the epistle. Knowledge in this sense is both an intellectual grasp of who God and Jesus are and what they say and demand, and a personal experience and commitment to them. Sometimes people these days will try and make a divide between so-called 'head knowledge' and 'heart knowledge'. While we all understand what they are saying, that sort of divide is most unbiblical. Often it becomes the excuse for some to avoid all serious Bible study for they want only to experience God in their hearts and feelings. Others, of course, at least in practice, tend to over-emphasise what we should *study* about God without drawing enough attention to experiencing the great joy of being his children.

Peter makes no such divisions, nor does any part of

Scripture. Here he states that Christians experience the grace of God and of Jesus and the objective reality of peace through the knowledge of God. Knowledge of God in the context of this letter clearly involves coming to know him personally and going through life experiencing his Spirit within, but also learning more about him through studying his Word more deeply. False teachers may have **known** the way of righteousness, but they have ignored it. It has not become part and parcel of their life and behaviour (2:20-21). The importance of what Peter says in verse 2 is dramatically emphasised as Peter closes his letter in 3:18 on the same note: **grow in the grace and knowledge of our Lord and Saviour Jesus Christ**. Unless we have a Christianity that is based on a knowledge of God revealed in his Word where we learn of him, and yet which is also rooted in a personal relationship that grows over the years, then we are liable to be led astray by false teachers. It is part and parcel of the Christian life this side of Christ's Second Coming that we are to continue growing in grace and the knowledge of God.

It is a common failing of Christians in all generations to think of themselves as something less than other Christians, or as having less by way of privilege. How good it is to know that we have what Peter and those early Jewish Christians had! We have a full equal standing in the covenant community within which we experience the grace and peace of God. A deeper knowledge of God will lead to a deeper experience of that continuing grace and peace even when faced with false teachers and the enemies of Christ.

2. Peter's gospel (1:3-11)

His divine power has given us everything we need for life and godliness through our knowledge of him who called us by his own glory and goodness. Through these he has given us his very great and precious promises, so that through them you

may participate in the divine nature and escape the corruption in the world caused by evil desires (verses 3-4).

What follows in verses 3-11 is rather like a complete summary of the apostle's teaching. It is almost as if Peter gives us the main headings of a sermon, as if he were saying, 'I am coming to the end of my life and I want you to remember the gospel. Remember what I have taught about God's wonderful grace that brings us knowledge of him, what I said about how to live for him, and of course about the eternal kingdom that awaits us all.'

The section can be divided into four: a) Christ has provided everything for salvation and life; b) Christ has made precious promises to us; c) the Christian must know how to respond; d) Christ promises the Christian a rich welcome and inheritance.

a) The gospel – Christ's provision (verse 3)

Peter now develops the need for continuing grace in the life of the believer. **His divine power has given us everything we need for life and godliness**. Here Peter refers to what Jesus has done for us. **His divine power** might refer to *God's* power, but in verse 16 Peter reminds his audience of the power of Christ that he witnessed at the Transfiguration. It thus makes sense to assume that Peter is talking of *Christ's* power, specially since Jesus was identified with God in verse 1. That verse also helps us know who the 'we' is to whom Peter refers. It could of course be the apostles, but after his insistence that his readers have received the same faith as the apostles, Peter is surely including them in what he is saying.

Christ's divine power not only called us to himself, but continues to supply **everything** that is necessary for us to be the Christians we should be. Christ supplies the wherewithal **for life and godliness**, in other words for the godly life all Christians should lead. This gracious supply of God is vital

even for forgiven sinners. They must rely continually upon
the source of life for continuing in that life. How good is the
Lord whose great and godly power is used to his people's
advantage to enable them to live for him!

'We' have been given all this, says Peter, **through our
knowledge of him who called us by his own glory and
goodness.** This develops his reference to 'knowledge' in verse
2. Coming to *know* Jesus is what happened at conversion,
but that knowledge continues to develop as we 'grow up' in
Christ. Although it is usually God who 'calls' in the New
Testament, there is no reason why Peter should not mean
Christ here, for it is his glory to which Peter refers in verse
17 and he is the one who is 'known' both in 1:2 and in 3:18.
So in coming to Christ and continuing to look to our
relationship with him (knowing him), we find that we have
been given everything we need for a godly life.

... **by his own glory** concerns the nature of Jesus himself.
Glory is a word that describes Jesus' divine character, a
character of **goodness** and love which was most clearly
demonstrated in the incarnation (see John 1:14, 'we have seen
his glory, the glory of the One and Only, who came from the
Father, full of grace and truth'.) But Christ's glory and
goodness have also been seen in his gracious calling of people
to himself as he carried out the will of the Father to save a
people for himself (John 17:3-5).

him who called us reminds us of the Saviour's initiating
work in our coming to faith. In the Old Testament it was
Israel whom God 'called' into being by his grace
(Deuteronomy 7:6-9). The word does not refer simply to an
outward call in the same way as I might call out to my son
and hope that he would come, but with no guarantee that he
will! Of course it can be used theologically in that way. For
example, an evangelist may issue a 'call' from the pulpit for
people to come to Christ in faith. In that sense people are

'called' and some will come and some will not. However, here the word is used with its full electing force. This is the sort of 'call' from the Saviour which is *effective*. It is the call which actually brings his covenant community into being. Peter picks up on this understanding of calling in verse 10 and refers to 'calling and election'.

b) The gospel – Christ's great promises (verse 4)
Through these he has given us his very great and precious promises ... Peter now says that **through these**, in other words, through Christ's 'own glory and goodness', he has given us **very great and precious promises**. What promises are these that we are so graciously given? Peter is clearly telling us that they are of great importance. In 3:13 Peter uses this rather rare word for 'promise' again and there it is a promise of **a new heaven and a new earth, the home of righteousness**. In chapter 3, verses 4 and 9, he has used a similar word. Again, in both cases Peter has in mind the future, specifically the return of Christ and all that will happen at that return.

This is surely what Peter means in these opening verses as well. Once we belong to Christ and 'know' him, we not only have all that we need to live this life in godliness, but we have set before us by Christ the most **precious** and **very great** promises for our future. Peter's sermonette here will end on a similar note in verse 11 by reminding us of the rich welcome into the eternal kingdom of Jesus Christ which awaits his people.

However, we may be limiting Peter's intention here too much if we say he is only referring to the future. In a very real sense Christians have already received the promises of Christ. We are already part of his holy people, sons and daughters of God, saved from the corruption of sin. In the next few verses Peter will go on to challenge his readers therefore to grow in God-like qualities which are already theirs.

Perhaps the best way of looking at these **precious promises**
is to remind ourselves that the fullness of Christ's glory and
goodness is yet to be experienced but we have already seen
and received a measure of it – what Paul calls the 'first-fruit'.
The over-riding context, however, is that we have a goal in
front of us and that is that we should be found fully mature in
Christ's eternal kingdom. That is a promise to us from Christ.[3]

The next part of this verse brings the thoughts together. ...
**so that through them you may participate in the divine
nature and escape the corruption in the world caused by
evil desires**. It is through the glory and goodness of Christ
and the most marvellous promises that he **has given us** that
we find ourselves able **to participate in the divine nature**.

At first sight this seems to be an extraordinary statement.
In an age like ours where many are involved in Eastern
religious ideas and New Age philosophies abound, we are
rightly cautious about anything that might suggest we become
'god' ourselves. The Bible always carefully maintains a
proper distinction between the Creator and his creation. It is
worth saying that Peter probably deliberately chose this rare
expression 'divine nature' because it would have been
recognised by his readers who had grown up in a pagan and
pantheistic environment.

What he is doing is re-defining, for those who have grown
up among such pagans, the way in which they might have
understood their relationship to God. They do not merge with
or become God. That is not Peter's point. However, in a very
real sense Christians do share in some of God's attributes,
not through effort or hard work, but through his grace. The
next part of the sentence helps us see just what Peter has in
mind. **... and escape the corruption in the world caused by
evil desires**. Christians are called to be 'holy' as God is holy,

---

3. Jesus promises his return and an eternal kingdom in a number of places in
the Gospels (e.g. Matthew 16:26, 27; 19:28; Luke 12:27-31; Mark 13:27 etc.).

a refrain repeated in Peter's first epistle (1 Peter 1:15, 16; 2:5). The apostle Paul can talk of Christians as 'sanctified in Christ Jesus and called to be holy' (1 Cor. 1:2). Christians do share in God's holiness and will one day be made perfect.

Christians also share in God's immortality. They are not trapped in this world. Though 'perishable' now, Christians will be raised 'imperishable' (1 Corinthians 15:42), and they will live forever.

Christians will even share in God's glory! It was this that Jesus so desired for his people as he prayed in John 17. Interestingly, in this prayer, Jesus uses somewhat similar ideas to those employed here by Peter. Note how in praying for his disciples Jesus points out the ways in which they are and will be like him, and then draws it together by talking of the unity between him and the Father and between him and his people. 'They are not of the world, even as I am not of it ... for them I sanctify myself, that they too may be truly sanctified. My prayer is not for them alone. I pray also for those who will believe in me through their message, that all of them may be one, Father, just as you are in me and I am in you. May they also be in us ... I have given them the glory that you gave me, that they may be one as we are one; I in them and you in me ...' (from John 17:16-23).

Through our knowledge of the Lord Jesus, our personal relationship with him, we are already one with Christ, and this has to be worked out in practice in this life, the point Peter makes in the second part of this sermonette. Indeed Christ's **divine power** enables us to be 'godly' in this life. However, the focus here is again on the future. Peter is aware that full holiness and immortality and glory await us in the 'eternal kingdom of our Lord'. In this sense Christians **participate in the divine nature** and will indeed **escape the corruption in the world caused by evil desires**.

It is worth saying here that Greeks would have seen escape

from evil and corruption in terms of escaping from the material world into some spiritual realm. Peter makes it clear that corruption in this world is caused by man's sinful desires. Christ has made it possible to escape evil and still live in and be part of this world.

These introductory verses have not been easy to follow. Peter uses a vocabulary that is both based in the Old Testament and yet adapted for his Greek audience, but the wonderful and thoroughly optimistic message rings through loudly into our age.

Christ is so very gracious that he hasn't just saved us and let us get on with life on our own. In his divine power he has given us all that we need to live a life worthy of him. He has done this for us as we have come to faith, to a knowledge of him. He has called us by his own glory and goodness and is even allowing us to participate in the divine nature as he shares various attributes with us including his glory, immortality and holiness.

It is good to pause before we look at Peter's exhortation in the next few verses, and consider the glorious truth and assurance that these verses contain for us as Christians. As we are tempted sometimes to despair of the evil around us, of our human frailty and ability to sin all too easily, let us remember that our salvation and knowledge of the Lord is entirely of grace. We do not have to strive by our own effort to remain within the love of God for he has supplied all that we need to live the life he wants of us. When we worry about our future or about what is in store for us, let us remember that Christ's divine power is carrying us forward to the time when we shall escape this world of sin and when the foretaste of the glory and goodness of Christ that we have now will be experienced in all its fullness.

c) The gospel – the Christian response (verses 5-9)

It is **for this very reason** that we are now expected to lead effective and productive lives. There is always an appropriate response to someone when given a precious gift. If it is someone close we may well throw our arms round them and give them a big hug. If it is someone a little further away from us, we may well write them a nice letter of thanks. In other cases we will see whether there is something we can give them or do for them. Underlying the whole of Christian life is this same principle. God and Jesus, our Saviour, have done so much for us that we long to be able to respond appropriately. But how? What could we ever bring to God that he would ever need? Nothing, of course.

Yet in his love and grace God has actually told us how he wants us to respond to his grace and love. It is summed up in the two great summary commands that Jesus gave us: ' "Love the Lord your God with all your heart and with all your soul and with all your mind and with all your strength." The second is this: "Love your neighbour as yourself"' (Mark 12:30-31). Peter is saying that, given Christ's extraordinary love for us in calling us to himself and allowing us to share in the divine nature, given his wonderful promises, it is **for this very reason** that we should develop personal qualities that will reflect the response that Jesus desires. Clearly it is significant that the list ends with the word 'love' in verse 7. That is the climax and summary of all the other qualities mentioned.

... make every effort to add to your faith goodness; and to goodness, knowledge; and to knowledge, self-control; and to self-control, perseverance; and to perseverance, godliness; and to godliness, brotherly kindness; and to brotherly kindness, love (verses 5-7). Perhaps after Peter's rehearsing of God's gracious activity in our lives it is strange to hear him say **make every effort**. But this is indeed what he says. Christians are to lead, first, an effective and productive

life and, secondly, they are to do this with effort and
eagerness.

First, an effective and productive life

We need to understand, here, that Peter is not going back on
his emphasis on grace but rather he has moved to talking of
our response to Christ's grace. What Christians should now
do as they seek to love God and their neighbour is to lead
effective and productive lives (verse 8), and this is a matter
of growth in our spiritual lives. It is interesting just how
important this concept is for Peter in this epistle. He uses the
verb form of the same Greek word for 'effort' in 1:10, and
1:15 and then summarises his epistle in 3:14 by saying: 'So
then, dear friends, since you are looking forward to this, make
every effort to be found spotless, blameless and at peace with
him.' It is only through growing spiritually and responding
to Christ more and more as we should that we will be able to
stand against false teachers and the temptations of sin. But
we also need to remember that Peter has already told us that
we shall achieve these qualities because **his divine power
has given us everything we need for life and godliness**.

As we learn from Paul in Galatians 5:22, it is the indwelling
presence of God's Holy Spirit that produces these 'fruit of
the Spirit'. In that passage Paul spells out for us this
relationship between the work of God and our own activity
in producing the fruit: 'Since we live by the Spirit, let us
keep in step with the Spirit.' The Christian life of response to
Christ means that we live by his Spirit, moving forward with
the **divine power** he has given us, and seeking to be the people
that we are called to be. We can state this in another way. We
must become, with God's help, the people we *are*. We are
God's people and so we must behave as God's people. As
Peter put it in 1 Peter 2:9: 'You are a chosen people, a royal
priesthood, a holy nation, a people belonging to God.' That

much is fact. It is not dependent upon our behaviour but upon
God's grace and the salvation of Jesus Christ. Nevertheless,
our response is to seek to be the people we now are, hence
Peter also says in 1 Peter 1:15: 'Just as he who called you is
holy, so be holy in all you do.'

i) *faith*

add to your faith goodness ... There is not an immediately
obvious progression here in the qualities that Peter lists and
perhaps we should not look for one. However, it is probably
significant that he starts with **faith** and of course summarises
it all with the final word **love**. Faith here is the gift from God
mentioned in verse 1 that allows us to trust in Christ and be
committed to him.

ii) *goodness*

It is this commitment aspect of faith that means it will always
be moving on and so Peter speaks of **goodness**. We have
already seen that goodness is one of the attributes of Jesus
(verse 3), and this whole process of growth is to become more
Christ-like, to become what we are: sharers in the divine
nature. We should live lives that are morally upright. How
often Christians are rightly criticised by those around for being
no better than anyone else. Our goodness should make us
stand out from the crowd!

iii) *knowledge*

This **knowledge** is not the same as that spoken of in verses 2
and 3. Here it has to do with the Christian's development of
an understanding and discerning mind: one that will see what
is good and God-honouring and one which can discern evil
and sin and so avoid it. This is a virtue that so often seems to
be lacking among Christians today. How many seem to be
able to pray each day 'Lead us not into temptation', and then
walk right into it!

iv) *self-control*

To the modern ear it may seem strange just how much attention is paid to **self-control** in the New Testament. In Acts 24:25 we see it was at the heart of the proclamation of the gospel for Paul: 'Paul discoursed on righteousness, self-control and the judgment to come.' Lack of self-control is listed as a mark of the evil of the last days in which we now live (2 Timothy 3:3). Sexual behaviour must exhibit self-control (1 Corinthians 7:5), and Paul again lists self-control among the fruit of the Spirit in Galatians 5:23. How different this way of life is to the life followed by the false teachers Peter will talk about in the next two chapters! They follow 'shameful ways' and are greedy (2:2-3), they are 'slaves of depravity' (2:19), and are 'following their own evil desires' (3:3).

Too often we see uncontrolled children these days. Their parents do not control them and they have never learned self-control. Many new Christians come from this sort of background and so find this particular virtue harder than many to achieve. Some of the older teens in the modern church are in just such a position in terms of drinking too much alcohol but also in their sexual lives, their language, their tendency to anger and so on. The challenge before them and all of us is both negative and positive. Not to be self-controlled is to follow the path of sin and one that false teachers all too readily hold before us, yet to be self-controlled is to open up one's life to Christian growth and joy, a right use of time and a life that brings glory to God.

v) *perseverance*

Perseverance has to do with remaining faithful in difficult times, withstanding temptation, and continuing on with the Lord. Again we need to remember that we do not persevere on our own. The Lord who began a work in us will carry it on to completion until the Day of Christ Jesus (Philippians 1:6). Indeed the doctrine of the *perseverance of the saints* is

one of the most marvellous doctrines of grace and the clearest
of evidences that salvation and even day to day life are a
matter of God's grace. However, again we are to put into
practice and work at this wonderful truth. Times of temptation
and trials and sufferings come to us all with astonishing
regularity. Perseverance therefore asks that we trust in God
and rely entirely on him at such times. It involves a total
practical commitment to the sovereignty of our Lord and
Saviour in our lives even when we are suffering. We are to
carry on in our faith to the very end, recognising that 'the
Lord knows how to rescue godly men from trials' (2:9).

vi) *godliness*

To perseverance we are to add **godliness**. In many ways this
is another all-embracing virtue. Godliness involves faith and
self-control, knowledge and goodness and so on. We noted
the word in verse 3 and here again we should remind ourselves
that we can attain even this for we have been **given everything
we need** to achieve this by coming to faith in Christ.

vii) *brotherly kindness*

As Peter nears the end of his list he talks of **brotherly
kindness**. 'Philadelphia' is the word used here, though I doubt
that the city of that name offers a particularly good example
of what Peter means here! This sort of Christian love is specially
aimed at the Christian community, our brothers and sisters
in the Lord. Paul tells us in Romans 12:10 to 'be devoted to
one another in brotherly love. Honour one another above
yourselves.' In 1 Thessalonians 4:9-10 Paul has to beseech
the church to love the brothers 'more and more'. Peter had
also made a point of stressing this Christian virtue in his first
epistle. In 1 Peter 1:22 he exhorted his readers to have a
'sincere love for your brothers ... from the heart'. In 1 Peter
3:8 he had called upon Christians to 'live in harmony with

one another; be sympathetic, love as brothers, be compassionate and humble'.

I know from my own childhood and from watching my own children, it often seems hardest to show our love to our brothers and sisters, even when we do really love them very much! Often this seems to be just as true in the Christian life. We really have to work at loving some people. Perhaps we do not get on, or agree with them. Perhaps they have hurt us in the past. There are lots of reasons why it may be hard to show real love for the Christian family, but learning to do this is a vital part of Christian growth. It is Jesus who stands before us again as not only the one who will help us do this by **his divine power** but also as the one who fully models what that love should really be all about: 'This is how we know what love is: Jesus Christ laid down his life for us. And we ought to lay down our lives for our brothers' (1 John 3:16).

Naturally, when people see this sort of brotherly love in action, it is most attractive. People are deeply drawn to a community where they see others truly caring for each other and loving each other. In an age of alienation, lack of love and loneliness, this can be one of the most attractive virtues of the Christian community, but it starts with us as individuals.

viii) *love*

Peter ends his list with **love**. This word, which Christ chose to summarise the whole law, calls upon us, heart, mind, soul and body, to set our affections on God the Father, Son and Holy Spirit, and to reflect the love of Christ to the world around us. With **faith** (and 'hope' not mentioned here) Paul reminds us that love lasts beyond the grave (1 Corinthians 13). Love is part of the **divine nature**.[4] It is therefore the ultimate 'mark' of a Christian.

---

4. 1 John 4:16 says, 'And so we know and rely on the love God has for us. God is love. Whoever lives in love lives in God, and God in him.'

For if you possess these qualities in increasing measure, they will keep you from being ineffective and unproductive in your knowledge of our Lord Jesus Christ (verse 8).

'What could I possibly do for the Lord?' is a question asked by so many Christians. Very often they are wrongly caught up with a world-view which believes that only ministers, priests, RE teachers, evangelists etc. can properly do anything for the Lord. I remember once hearing a very dynamic minister, speaking to a group of businessmen, suggest that unless they had given their testimony or spoken about the Lord to someone that day they had really wasted their time. No doubt we need to be reminded frequently to take advantage of any opportunity that God may give us to speak of him, but the whole theology of that minister was most unbiblical. God calls us to live for him wherever we are and to bring him glory as we live for him day by day in faith, goodness, self-control, godliness, love etc. In other words, we can bring glory to him by loving him in *every* area of our life. I have not at all wasted my time if, in the process of doing my normal routine job, I show forth self-control and godliness. I may not have spoken out evangelistically, but I have done what God most desires of me.

To learn increasingly how to live for the Lord and demonstrate the virtues appropriate to people who share the divine nature in any and every circumstance is, Peter says, what will **keep you from being ineffective and unproductive in your knowledge of our Lord Jesus Christ**. In other words, effectiveness and productivity in the Christian life is measured by the extent to which we are conformed more and more to the image of Christ himself, that is, by the extent to which we show forth the truth of our position that we **participate in the divine nature**.

For many people this is immensely tough as a challenge and yet wonderfully liberating as well. It allows us to be ourselves with our own personalities and gifts before God, and yet to know how we are to be and to live.

knowledge, here in verse 8, again reminds us that we shall never be satisfied as Christians for we shall always want to have a deeper relationship with our Saviour and to 'know' him better.

Sadly many Christians are not growing in this way and the contrast of verse 9 is telling indeed. **But if anyone does not have them, he is nearsighted and blind, and has forgotten that he has been cleansed from his past sins**.

We all know Christians, and perhaps we are sometimes among that number, who show few or none of these virtues that Peter has listed. As we noted earlier, this is all about living lives that are truly responsive to God's wonderful grace in the Lord Jesus Christ, so if we show none of these virtues, Peter is quite right to suggest that we must have forgotten that grace. Such a person is **nearsighted and blind**. A **blind** person can readily lose the way and to be **nearsighted** here implies that the person is unable to see what lies at the end of the way. The **nearsighted** person, in the sense that Peter is using the word here, is no doubt one who has lost all sense of the wonderful promises of God that have been mentioned earlier. This person cannot see beyond today and forgets that Christians are moving towards a goal. Not only is he unable to see the way ahead, but he must also have **forgotten that he has been cleansed from his past sins**.

The starting point for faith was coming to a knowledge of God and of Jesus Christ our Lord. This involved repentance and receiving God's forgiveness. All who do not seek to respond with love to the Lord who died to save them must indeed have forgotten what it cost Jesus to purchase his people's salvation and forgiveness.

This is a sobering challenge to us all. As we fail to grow in Christ, we not only become unproductive and lazy or ineffective Christians (verse 8) but we are also in effect saying by our lack of action: 'that forgiveness no longer matters to me.' Despising God's grace in our life and behaviour is quite unacceptable. And so Peter moves on to stress the need for an eagerness in the Christian life.

Second, eagerness and effort

Any Christian may be tempted to lose sight of the goal or forget the starting point of God's forgiveness and grace so Peter says: **Therefore, my brothers, be all the more eager to make your calling and election sure. For if you do these things, you will never fall ...** (verse 10)

As Peter nears the end of this sermonette and summary of his teaching, he does what every preacher does towards the end of a sermon, he makes the application explicit. **Therefore**, in other words because of what has been said, it is vital that these Christian **brothers** (men and women) to whom Peter is writing **be all the more eager**... Peter uses the verb form of a word he used back in verse 5. There it was translated 'make every effort', and this again is the thrust of Peter's message. The Christians in these churches must really work at their Christian faith.

I enjoy football, but I have to admit that it is a spectator sport for me. I usually watch the highlights of football matches late in the evening after a busy day at work. Many Christians treat their Christian faith in this way. It hardly, if at all, relates to their day to day life. At best it is something that involves them from the arm-chair at the end or the start of a busy day when they offer up a short prayer. Peter is adamant that there can be no 'arm-chair' Christians. Rather we must be **eager to make [our] calling and election sure**. The two words, **calling** and **election**, are closely related and both refer entirely to the gracious work of our sovereign Saviour in drawing Christians to himself. Initially this verse seems almost a contradiction in terms. We noticed this problem back in verse 5 as well. How does our work make certain something that is already certain because of God's gracious activity on our behalf?

Again we must not forget that Peter's sermon here began by reminding us of Christ's provision – that **his divine power has given us everything we need for life and godliness through our knowledge of him who called us ...** Peter is not therefore seeking to undermine a confidence in God's gracious work in a Christian's life, much the reverse. True Christians will, as noted earlier, be seeking to respond appropriately and from the heart to the grace and love of God. The law is now written on our hearts. Peter is reminding us in very stark terms that if we are recipients of God's grace then we shall be seeking to live the lives expected of the elect. Ultimately, of course, if a Christian has no desire to follow the life of obedience or to develop his or her life, the moral virtues of which Peter has been speaking, then he or she will **fall**. There is a response required of all who truly know and love the Lord Jesus and if that response is not seen then ultimate judgment awaits.

Of course, theologically, and based upon an understanding of God's grace in the life of a believer, we would be right to say that no one who is truly **called** and **elect** will ever **fall** in this final way. But that is not what Peter is concerned with here. His concern is to ensure that all Christians examine themselves. First, of course, they must ensure that they really do believe and trust Christ for everything, but, and here Peter is adamant, if they belong to Christ then their Christian growth towards holiness and godliness is vital and they will be held accountable.

Peter is not implying here that Christians can ever be perfect this side of eternity. He is not saying that they will never fail, or that they will always be fully self-controlled or always full of brotherly love, but he is saying that sure and certain Christian life will be working hard at these virtues continually, making use of the divine power given by Christ. Christians cannot do it on their own, but the Spirit within them will be driving all true believers towards the goal of a holy life.

It is wonderful to know that as we seek to grow as Christians and **do these things**, that is, live for God and make every effort to possess the qualities of which Peter has been speaking, that we will **never fall**, never lose our salvation. Rather Christians **will receive a rich welcome into the eternal kingdom of our Lord and Saviour Jesus Christ**.

d) The gospel – a rich welcome (verse 11)

The kingdom of God in Scripture refers to his rule and dominion. It is both present and future. Christ obviously has dominion and rule even over those who do not belong to him for he is their judge and they will stand before him at the Last Day. He is sovereign even in their affairs. However, the **eternal kingdom**, as Peter refers to it here, has in mind specially that dominion and rule of the Saviour which is part of the believer's most marvellous future inheritance. It is a wonderfully **rich** inheritance that will last through eternity for all the children of God. In 3:13 Peter summarises the essence of those great and rich blessings we shall gain as we are welcomed. He says **we are looking forward to a new heaven and a new earth, the home of righteousness**. Even there towards the end of his epistle he again adds, **So then ... make every effort to be found spotless ...** (3:14).

Many other passages of Scripture hint at what is in store for us in the new heaven and the new earth. For example in Revelation 21 we come to realise that the main wonder of the new revelation will be that God will be with his people and be their God, and there will be no more death or mourning or crying or pain. Peter's readers no doubt knew about this and so Peter does not delay on the nature of the inheritance of God's people at this point. He speaks only enough to remind us of where we are going, the joy that awaits us in the future and, therefore, just how important it is that we are the people we should be right now, this side of the eternal kingdom that we await.

Peter, regarding his own death as imminent, has given his readers a truly fascinating summary of the gospel he has taught. It gives us a challenging insight into some of what the apostles themselves saw as vital to the heart of the Christian faith. Peter spends time emphasising salvation by grace. But he moves on to speak of how the 'saved' life is to be lived, and that too is by grace, for Jesus has provided everything needed to live the godly life to which the believer is called. Nevertheless Christians are not machines. They have specific responsibilities to live out the lives to which they have been called and for which they have been empowered by the divine power, by Jesus and his Holy Spirit.

The dangers for all Christians are several and Peter is keen that we do not fall into any of the possible traps. We must never presume upon the grace of God. A virtuous and godly life is essential if we are to be the Christians we claim to be. The danger is that to miss out on such a life and to ignore the growth we ought to see as Christians, may lead to our falling and our condemnation at the last day. But our work here is always in the context of response to God who has so loved us. As we eagerly work for Christ in this context, so we shall be making clear to ourselves, to the world, and before God that our calling and election is sure. We really are the people we think we are!

The thrill and joy of what lies ahead of us outweighs any thought of hard work or difficulty in life. How much we should anticipate that wonderful rich welcome that awaits us, a welcome into **the eternal kingdom of our Lord and Saviour Jesus Christ.**

3. Remembering this gospel (1:12-21)
As Peter now continues we get a sense of increasing urgency, for he tells us of his imminent death.

> **So I will always remind you of these things, even though you know them and are firmly established in the truth you now have. I think it is right to refresh your memory as long as I live in the tent of this body, because I know that I will soon put it aside, as our Lord Jesus Christ has made clear to me. And I will make every effort to see that after my departure you will always be able to remember these things** (verses 12-15).

a) Remember – Peter will die soon (verses 12-15)
... as long as I live in the tent of this body does not indicate to us how close Peter's death was, but obviously he was awaiting it soon (**I will soon put it aside**). Interestingly he reminds his readers that his death was prophesied by the Lord himself. Perhaps some of the false teachers may have thought that Peter's impending death showed his lack of spirituality or a lack of real power that would enable him to escape. But Peter knows there are no promises to any Christians, even apostles, that they will not suffer in this world. Some will even be called upon to give their lives for faith in the Lord Jesus Christ. Peter was one of those and Jesus had mentioned it shortly after his resurrection at the end of John's Gospel. Jesus pushed Peter to express his love for him. Three times recalling Peter's earlier denials of Jesus, Jesus had asked whether Peter loved him. Peter had passionately reaffirmed his love for Jesus. Then Jesus added: 'Feed my sheep. I tell you the truth, when you were younger you dressed yourself and went where you wanted; but when you are old you will stretch out your hands, and someone else will dress you and lead you where you do not want to go' (John 21:17-18).

The reference to Peter's hands being 'stretched out' probably refers to death by crucifixion, but this is not certain. Tradition has it that Peter was crucified upside down because he would not allow them to crucify him in the same way as the Lord had been crucified. The evidence we have for this tradition, though, is late and we should not put much store by it. The important thing for us as we seek to understand what Peter was teaching, and his purpose in doing so, is to see that he knew he would shortly die and that this would be a fulfilment of the Lord's own prophecy to him.

Peter's attitude to his death is typical of the apostles and many faithful Christians down the centuries. He regards his life as being **in the *tent* of this body.** The physical body is but one part of our existence before God and it is temporary. Peter is not saying it is insignificant because of that, nor is he looking forward to a better spiritual state in which he will exist as a disembodied spirit. He of all people has seen the risen Lord Jesus and knows that a *real*, though different body awaits us at the *bodily* resurrection.[5] Rather here he is emphasising the fact that this life is temporary and passing. He is not so tied to this world and its possessions that he cannot bear the thought of passing on.

In our modern world we seem to find it increasingly difficult to keep our eyes focused on the future and the eternal kingdom. Often Christians are so caught up by their material possessions and a fairly easy-going life that they forget the very things of which Peter wishes to remind his readers here.

We can see immediately what Peter is concerned to do. In view of his death, he wants his readers to hold onto the whole gospel truth that he has preached to them during his life-time. He repeats three times (**I will always remind you** – verse 12; **I think it is right to refresh your memory** – verse 13; **I will make every effort to see that after my departure you**

5. See page 137, Appendix, New Heaven, New Body.

will always be able to remember these things – verse 15)
that he will remind them of these truths. Indeed this call to
remember is at the heart of the letter (see also 3:1 and 3:2).

This is not by any means new information for his readers.
Peter insists that the reminder of **these things** is given **even
though you may know them and are firmly established in
the truth** (verse12). They already knew all that he had spoken
of in verses 3-11. They knew of Christ's gracious provision.
They knew they had been forgiven and saved. They knew
that a response was required in the form of a godly life. They
knew they had Christ's power within to help them in day to
day life. And they knew of the rich welcome and eternal
kingdom that awaited them. All of this was standard gospel
teaching and these Christians both knew the truth of the
teaching and were also firmly established in it. Yet still they
needed 'reminding'.

Peter is not so much concerned about whether they
remember the facts of the faith. His concern is that these facts
continue to make a difference in their lives as they live for
Christ. In this sense he asks these Christians to remember, in
the same way as all Christians need to keep remembering,
the core of the gospel. It is so easy in Christian life, specially
if there are some false teachers around as there were in this
church, to move away from the root of the faith. The apostle
Paul had been faced with a similar issue as he wrote 1
Corinthians. The Corinthians thought they had moved on to
'deeper' things! They thought they were spiritually mature,
while Paul had to remind them 'I resolved to know nothing
while I was with you except Jesus Christ and him crucified.'
For Paul this was a short-hand way of talking of the core
gospel which Peter has just summarised.

In Christian life there is a continual need to 'remember' in
this way. That's why Peter says **always** here in verse 12 and
'at all times' in verse 15 (NIV, **always**). Christians may not

forget the factual teaching about Christ's death, but all of us can so easily forget the implications of that message for how we live and how we are. No Christian has the right to 'forget' (verse 9) the gospel core of Christ's gracious work for us. The more we remember all that Christ has done for us and continues to do for us then the better we will live for him and the more we will seek to respond in love and obedience.

In instituting the Lord's Supper, our Lord recognised this continual need that Christians have of remembering Christ's work for us and the whole of the gospel message. Let us never imagine that just because we are **firmly established in the truth** which we **know**, that we have arrived or that we can move onto other things at the expense of the very heart of the gospel. This is just what false teachers would have us believe. They will sell their teachings on the basis of 'moving on' or 'going deeper'. To his readers, and to us across the centuries, who live so long after his **departure**, Peter says remember **these things**. Peter may not have had long to live, but in writing his epistle he achieved his objective of ensuring people did indeed 'remember' and thus continued in future generations to live godly lives for Christ in the face of all kinds of persecution and false teaching.

b) Remember – because the apostles were witnesses (verses 16-18)

We did not follow cleverly invented stories when we told you about the power and coming of our Lord Jesus Christ, but we were eye-witnesses of his majesty (verse 16).

Having summarised the gospel he preached in verses 3-11 and concluded that section talking of the future, Peter now returns to this most important aspect of Christian teaching: the Second Coming of our Lord. The way he tackles the subject here and then returns to it at greater length at the end of the epistle suggests that it was one of the doctrines criticised by or misrepresented by the false teachers. Indeed, Peter's move at this point from 'I' to 'we' suggests he was confronting a full blown attack on this aspect of apostolic teaching.

Certainly the Second Coming of Christ figured prominently in both apostolic teaching generally, but also in the small amount of Peter's own preaching that has come down to us in Acts. Of course, in a book like Acts we only have the highlights of what Peter would have said. But even so, we can see that the Second Coming was a central part of what Peter taught. In the sermon recounted from the Day of Pentecost the reference to the Second Coming is only implicit with mention of the 'great and glorious day of the Lord' and the need for salvation (2:20-21). But in Acts 3:19-21 Peter preaches: 'Repent, then, and turn to God, so that your sins may be wiped out ... and that he may send the Christ, who has been appointed for you – even Jesus. He must remain in heaven until the time comes for God to restore everything, as he has promised long ago through his holy prophets.' In Acts 10:42 Peter explains to Cornelius that the apostles had been commanded to preach that Christ had been appointed judge of the living and dead. Then, of course, this teaching was of vital importance to Peter's first epistle where, in the opening verses, he reminds the readers 'of the coming salvation that is ready to be revealed in the last time' (1 Peter 1:5; see also 1 Peter 4:4-7, 13; 5:1, 4)

Just what people were saying against this teaching is not clear. Nevertheless, the formidable nature of the attack on the **very great and precious promises** is made somewhat clearer elsewhere in the epistle. Peter argues in these immediate verses that it is not he and the other apostles who have invented things. Then, in 2:1 he insists it is the false teachers who in fact have introduced heresies and who have made up stories with which to exploit Christians (2:3). Peter spends some time warning of examples of God's judgment and salvation in the rest of chapter 2, reminding his readers that Christ will return to judge. In 3:3-5 he outlines clearly that these false teachers deliberately 'forget' the teaching of God's creation and scoff at those who suggest Jesus will return. Peter reminds his readers again in that section of what Christ has done, of what he has promised and demonstrates just how false these teachers really are.

Perhaps the false teachers were so influenced by their pagan Greek-thinking environment that they objected to teachings about the Second Coming, and judgment after death, and refused to accept the idea of divine sovereignty in history. For example, Epicureans were noted for their emphasis on 'freedom' in which they affirmed that human sensations, preconceptions and feelings were the standard of truth and that the end of all action was to be free from pain and fear. Teachers of this school of thought were particularly scathing in their attack on what they regarded as 'myths', specially 'myths' that concerned future worlds and judgment. Although we cannot be certain that this was what was being taught by the false teachers, it seems that something of the sort was probably causing the serious problem Peter confronts, for he insists that what he and the apostles taught were not 'stories' ('myths' in Greek). And later in chapter 2 he spends some time insisting that God will indeed return to judge in the future as he has judged in the past.

However, here in chapter 1 Peter vehemently insists on the genuine nature of the original apostolic gospel concerning Christ's return.

First, we need to note that Peter makes it clear the apostles did not differ in what they taught as 'Gospel'. As a group they had taught what Peter had just summarised and they had all taught the truth of Christ's coming.

Secondly, they had taught of the power and coming of our

Lord Jesus Christ (verse 16). Unlike the false teachers who really were making up stories to lead people into heresy, the apostles truthfully and accurately recounted the teachings of Jesus. This included relating the **power** of Christ's Second Coming. Many references in the Bible to Christ's Second Coming portray something of his great power. This includes his power to save for eternal life and his power to judge to eternal death. Jesus himself, drawing closely on the teaching of the Old Testament and applying it to himself, made this point in Mark 13:26-27: 'At that time men will see the Son of Man coming in clouds with great power and glory. And he will send his angels and gather his elect ...' (see also Matthew 24:30-35; 25:31-32).

Interestingly, Peter now recalls the Transfiguration to argue that the Second Coming has the backing of apostolic eye-witness. This great event had left a lasting impression upon him. This was the time when he and James and John saw Jesus 'transfigured' – **we were eye-witnesses of his majesty. For he received honour and glory from God the Father ...** (verses 16-17).

There had been no greater evidence during Jesus' whole life-time of both his power and his majesty than this episode recounted for us in Matthew 17:1-8, Mark 9:2-8 and Luke 9:28-36. In all three Gospels the episode is placed in the context of Jesus beginning to teach his disciples that he would have to suffer and die. What the disciples were being taught was that through the suffering, death and resurrection of Jesus lay the route to glory. The Second Coming of Jesus would be fundamentally different from his first coming. Instead of humbling himself and limiting the exercise of his divine attributes, instead of coming to suffer and die, his return would be as sovereign Lord and king with full power and majesty.

The Transfiguration, therefore, offered the disciples a foretaste of that glory. It offered them, as it were, a glimpse through to the future, through suffering and death and resurrection and into Christ's glorification. It would be as the glorified Lord that he would return. Thus, for Peter and the apostles, the experience became evidence of the risen Christ and thus the returning Christ. This amazing insight was given by Jesus as a special privilege to Peter, James and John.

For he received honour and glory from God the Father when the voice came to him from the Majestic Glory, saying ... (verse 17). The words **honour** and **glory** naturally hang together. 'Glory' is a word that is specially linked with Christ's Second Coming in the Gospels of Matthew, Mark and Luke. But right back in Psalm 8:5[6] the two words ('honour' and 'glory') are seen together in a Messianic Psalm emphasising how man has been made ruler over all and given authority. That psalm is taken up and applied to Christ in Hebrews 2:7-9 who now has all authority and is crowned with 'glory and honour'. What Peter is thus stressing is that the words of the Father helped the apostles see the kingly divine rule of Christ which was yet to come.

For Peter the words of the heavenly Father were thus deeply significant in confirming the majesty of the one transfigured before them in a context where they had been thinking about his suffering and death. The significance of these particular words becomes even more evident as we examine them. Peter recalls them: **This is my Son, whom I love; with him I am well pleased**. These are virtually the same words as we find in Matthew 17:5.[7] In using these words the Father is alluding to two Old Testament texts full of meaning in their own right.

---

6. In the Greek version, the LXX.
7. The Greek of Matthew and 2 Peter are very slightly different. There are also slight variations between the words the Father speaks in the three Gospels, but they are not of great significance in terms of the points Peter makes. Mark leaves out 'with him I am well pleased' as does Luke. Luke has 'whom I have chosen' rather than 'whom I love'.

The first is Psalm 2:7. Again this is known as a 'Messianic Psalm' for here God the Father speaks to the Son who will come to rule the nations: 'He said to me, "You are my Son; today I have become your Father." ' This, in turn, recalls the wonderful covenant that God made with David in 2 Samuel 7:14 in which God promises that one day a king will sit on David's throne who will rule for ever and he says: 'I will be his father, and he shall be my son ... my love will never be taken away from him.' God's assertion at the Transfiguration that 'This is my beloved Son' was thus identifying Jesus as the Davidic (Messianic) king of covenant love and promise.

The background to the second part of the statement – **with him I am well pleased** – is also fascinating. This is drawn from Isaiah 42:1 which speaks of the Suffering Servant, but also points to the servant's role in bringing justice to all the nations: 'Here is my servant, whom I uphold, my chosen one *in whom I delight*; I will put my Spirit on him and he will bring justice to the nations.' The allusion makes it clear that the Father was stressing that this Jesus was the one he had chosen to be the king. Jesus' calling and work, including his future role of judgment, was all part of the Father's will.

So why is the Transfiguration such vital evidence to the Second Coming? Well, Peter continues: **We ourselves heard this voice that came from heaven when we were with him on the sacred mountain**. Here surely is the key to what Peter is writing. The important thing about the Transfiguration lies in both what the apostles *saw*, and in what they *heard*. They had seen the glory of the Son, but they had also heard God the Father from his Majestic Glory identifying this Jesus as the one appointed to be king and to fulfil the role of authority and judgment over the nations spoken of in Psalm 2:6-9. That Peter has this in mind is further indicated by his mention of **the sacred mountain**, a phrase which appears in very similar Greek form (LXX) in Psalm 2:6.[8]

Peter thus calls people to remember God's truth, the gospel, specially the Second Coming, because of what the apostles had heard and seen in the Transfiguration. They saw that Jesus was the Son, the long promised and long awaited King of glory and ruler of the world. They had heard that he was both Servant and Judge. That day of the Transfiguration had been a foretaste of Christ's glory, rule, power and honour. Christ had not yet been seen again in this way, therefore it is clear that the Second Coming is still awaited. At that time the prophecies surrounding the king in the specific passages to which the Father had referred would indeed come to pass.

c) Remember – because Scripture can be trusted (verses 19-21)

> **And we have the word of the prophets made more certain, and you will do well to pay attention to it, as to a light shining in a dark place, until the day dawns and the morning star rises in your hearts** (verse 19).

The *spoken* words of the heavenly Father had been the key for Peter to understanding the Transfiguration, but even those words of the Father had pointed back to Scripture. It is to this *written* word that Peter now turns for his second line of evidence for the Second Coming.

i) *Pay attention to Scripture*
we have still refers, as in verse 16 to the apostles themselves. The apostles have been teaching that Christ will return. Among the evidences for this are the Transfiguration and the **word of the prophets**. More than likely, Peter is here thinking of the whole Old Testament as the prophetic word, but he is specially interested at this moment in passages which talk of

---

8. Psalm 2:6, LXX – 'I have been made king by him on Zion his holy mountain.' The LXX is the Greek version of the Old Testament that would have been known in Peter's day.

Christ's return to judge and to save. **made[9] more certain** has
caused a great deal of discussion among commentators.
Simply the issue is 'more certain than what?' Surely, Peter
would not imply that the prophets were more certain than the
apostles in what they said! Perhaps the best way of
understanding this is that the apostles' teaching about the
coming of Jesus, based upon the Transfiguration and the
words of God the Father, is still further authenticated by the
sure word of prophecy. In other words, Peter is not comparing
one evidence against another as if one might be more
convincing, but is simply adding one evidence on top of
another. Both the witnesses are definite and reliable, but
together they will persuade still further any who might have
been tempted to doubt by the false teachers.

The prophetic word of (Old Testament) Scripture is utterly
to be trusted and so Peter says, **you will do well to pay
attention to it**. Time and again the Old Testament speaks of
God returning to judge and on many occasions it becomes
clear that it is the Messiah, the son of David, who will carry
out that judgment. Though the Messiah has now come, it is
self-evident that he has not yet returned in glory and brought
judgment to the nations, and so there is ample prophecy, to
which Christians must pay attention, that speaks of Christ's
Second Coming.

God's truth in Scripture shines out in a dark age, **as a light
shining in a dark place**. We understand the picture all too
well for it so aptly describes the world as we know it now. It
is a world full of uncertainties, and in which people are
desperately trying to discover what the future holds.
Horoscopes, the occult, New Age religions, strange religious
sects are all symptoms for us of an age that still struggles in
darkness. Christians, on the other hand, have revelation, God's
own word on the matter, and it is to be trusted and listened

---

9. This word is not found in the Greek.

to. God's word offers us a firm and solid foundation for living in this world where ignorance of God's word and therefore of the future leaves people lost in darkness. Even though we do not as yet 'see face to face' (1 Corinthians 13:12), and even though we do not understand all that will happen when Christ returns, Christians do have God's word on the matter. The Son will return to judge those who have rejected him and to save those who belong to him by grace through faith.

Recently my son bought a very strong halogen torch (flashlight). It is truly extraordinary what a couple of batteries and such a small bulb will do in lighting up a dark room or even the dark garden at night. This is Peter's description here of God's Word, and it is reminiscent of Psalm 119:105: 'Your word is a lamp to my feet and a light for my path.' Scriptures light our way **until the day dawns**. In other words, the truth we do have is enough. It tells us of salvation in Christ and provides us with the precious promises of God and a sure and certain knowledge, not of the detail, but certainly of the fact of Christ's Second Coming. Paul uses a similar picture to describe this age between the first and second comings of Christ. In Romans 13:11-13 he talks of 'understanding this present time.... The night is nearly over; the day is almost here. So let us put aside the deeds of darkness ...'

and the morning star arises in your hearts takes Peter's thoughts a step further. By talking of the 'morning star' Peter is probably recalling Numbers 24:17 which is another 'messianic prophecy'. There we read: 'A star will come out of Jacob; a sceptre will arise out of Israel. He will crush the foreheads of Moab ...' Again the context talks of judgment that will be brought to the nations by one of the descendants of Jacob. But this morning star, Jesus, will not produce fear in the hearts of his followers. Rather they will finally know Jesus fully and their hearts (and whole lives) will be filled with joy.

Peter's insistence here that his readers must pay attention to Scripture, to the prophetic word, is very important for us today. Together with Peter's audience, we too live in anticipation of the Second Coming. If ever we are tempted to doubt this, as Peter's readers were, then we must remember that *the Second Coming is part and parcel of the gospel message preached by the apostles*. They saw the glorified Christ in all his majesty and they also heard the Father himself give honour and glory to the Son. The prophetic word (Old Testament teaching) is also quite certain on the point.

The apostles taught this truth, not as an optional extra, but as part of the core gospel. From this truth come all sorts of other important lessons for Christ's church. One of the most important is that, having this light shining in a dark place means we must live as people of the light. In other words, as we look forward to Christ's return we behave now as people who are awaiting him (Romans 13:12-13; Philippians 2:15-16). In Peter's terms we must **be all the more eager to make our calling and election sure** so we **will receive a rich welcome into the eternal kingdom**. Perhaps we all need to ask ourselves again just how much we consider the Second Coming of the Lord to be 'core Gospel' – that is relevant to us day by day. Certainly Bible-believing Christians trust that Christ will return, but to what extent do we live in the light of the truth and to what extent do we let it govern our lives, for it is no less than this that Peter wants of us?

ii) *The authority of Scripture*
Above I have assumed that the word of the prophets (verse 19) refers to the whole of Scripture and that Scripture is God's Word and therefore true because 'God does not lie' (Titus 1:2). This is precisely how Peter wanted us to take his teaching here. That word is a **light shining in a dark place**, and God is light (1 John 1:5). As Isaiah said when speaking of that future coming of the Lord: 'the LORD will be your everlasting

light, and your God will be your glory' (Isa. 60:19-20). Peter wants us to know that what the prophets say is what God says and thus to be trusted and believed.

However, because there is an argument going on here with the false teachers who say all talk of Christ's return is no more than myth or story (verse 16), Peter re-emphasises just what authority the 'prophets', the writers of Scripture, really did have.

> **Above all, you must understand that no prophecy of Scripture came about by the prophet's own interpretation. For prophecy never had its origin in the will of man, but men spoke from God as they were carried along by the Holy Spirit** (verses 20-21).

These verses give us some indication of the sort of arguments that may have been used against the apostolic teaching. Perhaps the false teachers were saying something like this: 'the prophets spoke for themselves and wrongly interpreted events. Indeed some of them simply made up their own prophecies – a creation of their all too clever minds.' Of course, we cannot know for certain that this is what they were saying for we have only Peter's response to look at.

Above all, you must understand is a phrase that recurs in 3:3 and indicates that Peter considers what he is about to say to be vital. Indeed what follows is the main thought of the sentence which concludes at the end of verse 20: **no prophecy of Scripture came about by the prophet's own interpretation**. Once again there is a problem as to just what Peter means here. The Revised Standard Version captures the Greek more literally: 'no prophecy of scripture is a matter of one's own interpretation'. The New International Version interprets 'one's own' as the 'prophet's own'. In other words Peter may be suggesting either that no prophecy in Scripture is a matter of the reader's own interpretation in the present or that the origin of prophecy lay not with the prophet's own understanding but was directly from God. The latter is the

New International Version's understanding and probably
makes the best sense of the verse which then leads naturally
into verse 21: **For prophecy never had its origin in the will
of man but men spoke from God as they were carried along
by the Holy Spirit**.

Peter is insisting on the full authority of Scripture because
the origin of all that is said by the prophets is from the Holy
Spirit. Against all who would say otherwise, Peter argues
that the prophets were not simply making up something to fit
the times, to interpret an experience or to make a point based
upon their own assessment of the situation. Rather the
prophets were **carried** or 'borne along' by the Holy Spirit so
that what they **spoke** was **from God**.[10]

Peter thus brings to a close this section of his letter in which
he has forcefully defended the truth of all that the apostles
had taught concerning the Second Coming. The
Transfiguration offered clear evidence that Christ would
return in glory and the apostles had been eye-witnesses of
this event. They had *seen* the glory but they had also *heard*
the Father's words on the matter. Further evidence of the
truth of what they have taught about the Second Coming is
to be found in the Scriptures which look forward to the day
of judgment and salvation. Lest any should doubt that the
word of prophecy was utterly to be trusted, as the false
teachers seem to have done, Peter then insists that the men
who wrote Scripture were carried along by the Holy Spirit.
In other words what **men spoke** was indeed the message of
God himself, fully inspired by the Holy Spirit.

Peter thus defends apostolic truthfulness and God-given
authority and Old Testament authority. He will return to the
word of the prophets and of the apostles as he again picks up
the theme of the last days in 3:2 – 'I want you to recall the

---

10. It is of interest that the same Greek verb for 'borne' is used for God's
voice being heard in verse 18, which was 'borne from heaven' (RSV).

words spoken in the past by the holy prophets and the command given by our Lord and Saviour through your apostles.'

Special Lessons for Today

We have already mentioned how central the Second Coming must be to the thinking of the modern-day mature Christian. As Peter has developed a defence of apostolic teaching on this matter, however, he has opened up for his readers a discussion about *authority*. His readers would have to decide whether to listen to the apostles or to the false teachers they had around them. This question of *authority* is one which causes the modern church enormous problems. As we see from this epistle, these problems are nothing new, but we avoid or ignore them at our peril. Just as Peter forced his readers to face the issue head on (i.e. the apostles and Scripture or the thinking of the age), so we must do the same.

The apostle Paul talked of the church being 'built on the foundation of the apostles and prophets, with Christ Jesus himself as the chief cornerstone' (Ephesians 2:20). As we commit ourselves to the Creator God and the Lordship of Christ, we do so on the basis of the teaching of the Scripture which comes to us through 'prophets' and 'apostles'. It is important to realise that without this authoritative teaching of Scripture, we will have a Jesus of our own creation, one who is indeed simply a matter of 'one's own' interpretation. Given that virtually everything we know about Jesus comes from Scripture and given that Christians have committed themselves to the Lordship of Christ based on *biblical* evidence, it is vital that we also take seriously Scripture's own claims about itself. Peter has told us that it has been written by those who were borne along by the Holy Spirit. The Holy Spirit has so overseen the work of these men that what they have written, though truly in their own words and style, is indeed the Word of God and therefore carries *God's* full authority.

It is important for us to understand that a commitment to the true Christ revealed in Scripture, rather than a mythological Christ of our imagination, requires some level of commitment to the authority of Scripture. The apostle Paul pulls this together for us in 2 Timothy 3:15-16 where he shows that it is the *Scriptures* which have opened the way for faith in Christ and then leads into a discussion of their inspiration and authority: '... from infancy you have known the holy Scriptures, which are able to make you wise for salvation through faith in Christ Jesus. All Scripture is God-breathed ...'. It is interesting to reflect on the fact that Paul's discussion in that letter also arises, as we have found in 2 Peter, in a context dealing with false teachers who want to communicate more acceptable and enticing doctrines that are not from God.

Many these days think that it is possible to have a full commitment to Christ but not to Scripture. While I would not doubt that people can come to have a full heart commitment to Christ as Lord and Saviour and yet have an inadequate view of the authority of Scripture, it is important to see that such a stance is riddled with inconsistencies and reflects a desperate need to mature in the faith. If Scripture comes from the Holy Spirit as Peter and Paul affirm, then on what basis can we say we accept some parts and not others? Usually parts of Scripture are simply denied because they are not compatible with what we want to hear in the twentieth century! Now, of course, I do not mean to minimise the need for careful study and interpretation to see just exactly what Scripture is really saying. I do not deny that God used very different literary *genres* to communicate his will to us and that each one will be interpreted in somewhat different ways. Nevertheless, when we believe we know what Scripture is affirming in the passage we are studying, we are required to treat that as the Word of God inspired by the Holy Spirit. It is interesting to see that our doctrine of Scripture is ultimately dependent, therefore, upon our doctrine of God. If what we have before us is from God, then just as God cannot lie (Titus 1:2) surely his word does not lie.

Some who do treat Scripture as 'authoritative' suggest that this does not mean the Bible is therefore 'without error' or 'inerrant' to use the fairly recent jargon. For example, in some places, they say, it will reflect the inadequate time-bound thinking of a writer too caught up in his own culture. This is a very common view in some circles these days. It is immediately attractive. Essentially the Bible is true, but not necessarily in the detail. Of course it is true when dealing with salvation and judgment, with the need for repentance and forgiveness, when telling us about Jesus and God, but on other matters of less importance it may or may not be reflecting the mind of God.

Again, though, we need to ask who the arbiter will be on whether some Scripture is of God and some not. Who is the arbiter of what is important and what is not? What is fascinating in Scripture is how apparently insignificant details are later picked up in a very significant manner. For example, one cannot help being impressed by the arguments of the apostle Paul in Romans where apparently small details of dates surrounding events in Abraham's life become part of the argument for justification by faith (Romans 4).

It seems to me that the traditional view of orthodox Christianity down through the ages, that Scripture is to be trusted throughout as God's word, is consistent with the evidence of Scripture itself and of how God speaks to his people. The fact that we often find some parts of Scripture not at all to our liking or very difficult to understand is an indication that we do not yet see 'face to face' but still have a long way to grow and mature in **the grace and knowledge**

of our Lord and Saviour Jesus Christ (2 Peter 3:18).

It is important to say one more thing on this matter of the authority and inspiration of Scripture. For those of us who do believe Scripture is without error in all that it affirms, there remains the great danger that our practice does not conform to our doctrine. Christian life is about being more and more conformed to the mind of Christ which we find in Scripture. But so often we are tempted to walk in an altogether different direction! Theoretical knowledge of the truth without obedience is never sufficient for Christian life and service of the Lord. We may make all the right noises about the authority of Scripture and we may stand up well against false teachers, but of what value is it to us personally if, knowing the will of God and his truth, we do not then obey it?

4. Beware of false prophets and teachers (2:1-10a)

Chapter divisions are often rather arbitrary in the Bible and here is a clear example. The words **But** and **also** of the first verse help us understand that Peter is developing the same train of thought. He has been speaking about the truthful testimony to the gospel, to Christ and to the Second Coming which is to be found in the message of the apostles and in the writings of the Old Testament prophets. They have spoken the mind and will of God on the matter. The apostles were able to do so because they had seen the glorified Lord and heard the Father pronounce on the matter. The writers of the Old Testament were able to do so because they had been moved by the Spirit of God to record and speak out the mind of God. Peter has thus defended biblical authority and the specific content of the message which has been challenged by false teachers (1:16).

a) They teach heresies (verse 1)

Having defended his position and re-emphasised the centrality
to the gospel of the Second Coming, Peter now moves on to
the attack. Not all prophets can be trusted for, just as in the
past, there are and will be false prophets and false teachers
around and this is the problem for the Christians to whom
Peter is writing and the issue which he now addresses.

> **But there were also false prophets among the people, just as
> there will be false teachers among you. They will secretly
> introduce destructive heresies, even denying the sovereign
> Lord who bought them — bringing swift destruction on
> themselves** (Verse 1).

During the whole history of God's people there have been
false teachers and false prophets. It is to this that Peter first
draws attention, **there were also false prophets among the
people.** The true prophets of old such as Jeremiah, Ezekiel
and Zechariah forcefully warned of the great danger of such
people. For example, in Jeremiah 23:16-17 we read, 'This is
what the LORD Almighty says: "Do not listen to what the
prophets are prophesying to you; they fill you with false
hopes. They speak visions from their own minds, not from
the mouth of the LORD. They keep saying to those who despise
me, 'The LORD says: You will have peace.' And to all who
follow the stubbornness of their hearts they say, 'No harm
will come to you.' " '[11] The characteristic traits of those false
prophets were usually the same, and are well reflected in those
whom Peter will go on to attack in this chapter: i) they would
scorn and pour contempt on God's true prophets; ii) they
would invent visions and dreams in order to deceive God's
people; and iii) they would deliberately deny any prospect of

---

11. See also Jeremiah 14:14, Ezekiel 13:1-12 and Zechariah 13:2-5. Ezekiel
specially highlights that these false prophets recount false visions (verse 6)
and they offer 'peace when there is no peace' (verse 10).

God's imminent judgment.[12] It is also characteristic of the passages dealing with false prophets in the Old Testament that their judgment by God is certain.

So Peter has this background in mind as he continues **just as there will be false teachers among you**. No doubt Peter knows that this will always be a problem for God's people until Christ returns in glory but, as he writes, he may have in mind some specific prophecies about false teachers[13] in the church that he had heard from the mouth of the Lord himself. This is particularly likely when we read 3:1-4. There Peter asks his readers to remember both the words of the prophets of the past and the Lord's own words that have come through the apostolic teaching.

The Lord himself had urged his disciples on a number of occasions to take note of the existence of false prophets. In Matthew 7:15 we read of Jesus saying, 'Watch out for false prophets. They come to you in sheep's clothing, but inwardly they are ferocious wolves.' And in Matthew 24:11 and 24 he again speaks on the matter: 'many false prophets will appear and deceive many people.... For false Christs and false prophets will appear and perform great signs and miracles to deceive even the elect – if that were possible.' In view of Peter's comments about the apostle Paul in 3:15, it is also possible he had in mind some of Paul's warnings. For example, in 2 Thessalonians 2:1-3 the apostle Paul had also

---

12. One of the most notable examples of this happening in practice is seen in 1 Kings 22:1-28. Here God's prophet Micaiah foretells the downfall of King Ahab. Ahab's own prophets had all foretold victory in battle for Ahab. Micaiah at one point even tells Ahab what he wants to hear, but Ahab doesn't actually believe him (verses 15-16)!

13. Some commentators see a significance in Peter's moving from talk of false 'prophets' to false 'teachers' here. The change may simply be stylistic, or it may be that these evil people were not actually calling themselves 'prophets' on this occasion. Either way, the words of the true prophets, and of the Lord and of the apostles are all directly relevant to the false teachers whom Peter confronts.

spoken of the possibility of a false prophecy specifically with regard to the Second Coming and had urged people not to be deceived.[14] Apostolic warnings no doubt abounded as Jude 17 makes clear.[15]

The future tense continues as Peter reminds his readers of these prophecies: **They will secretly introduce destructive heresies**. The word 'heresy' does not carry with it the fully developed meaning it has in modern English of a set of teachings that are wrong and pitted against orthodoxy. Rather the word can simply refer to a particular, perhaps variant, teaching. For example, it is used in Acts 24:5 of the Nazarene 'heresy' which the New International Version rightly translates 'sect'. This is why Peter qualifies the word. What these false teachers will teach are not permissible 'variants' but rather **destructive heresies**. Furthermore these will be secretly introduced. This will always be the way of false prophets and teachers, so there can be no grounds for complacency.

– bringing swift destruction on themselves. Notice Peter's double irony as he comments upon the end of their work: **they bring swift destruction on themselves!** A person, whose teaching is *destructive* to God's people, will be *destroyed* by God. And, in spite of their insistence that **everything goes on as it has since the beginning of creation** (3:4), the fact is that God's destruction is imminent! Peter will develop the certainty of their condemnation from verse 4 onwards in this chapter.

---

14. See also Acts 20:29-31. It is particularly interesting that in 2 Timothy, a letter probably written around the time 2 Peter was written, Paul confronts again the issue of false teachers. Specially see 2 Timothy 4:3-5. There is no doubt that, towards the end of their lives, both Peter and Paul became increasingly concerned about false teachers. Hence of course Peter's ambition to see that his warnings are heard beyond his death (2 Peter 1:15).

15. If 2 Peter was written after Jude then it is at least possible that Peter was actually drawing on Jude's warnings in this epistle.

He singles out the fact that they are **even denying the sovereign Lord**. Here the overlap with Jude (verse 4) is obvious. But, as we said in the Introduction, we cannot be sure whether one writer borrowed from the other or whether both borrowed from some other source. Whatever the truth of the relationship between the two epistles, both writers are concerned about people who deny the Master.

In both epistles the word appearing in the New International Version as 'Sovereign Lord' is *despotes* which might better be translated 'Master'. This rare word brings to mind the picture of slaves with a master. Slaves have to obey their master or suffer the consequences. In the Christian faith there is a commitment to Christ as the covenant Lord who demands our obedience. By using the word 'Master' in this way Peter may be drawing attention to this aspect of what the false teachers are saying. They are leading people away from obedience and the **way of truth** (verse 2) to follow **their [own] shameful ways**.

Although Jude should not dictate our understanding of what Peter says here, it is worth noting that Jude directly links this denial of the Master to the licentious behaviour of the false teachers. In that context 'denial' seems to mean that they are *living* a denial. In other words, they are denying the Master by not obeying him and living as he has commanded.

The denial of the Master to which Peter is referring could be a reference to their denial of his Second Coming or, since Peter immediately talks of their **shameful ways** and later of their immorality, it could be this to which he is referring. Either is possible and perhaps both are in Peter's mind. Christ's sovereign Lordship is denied in practice if people refuse to heed God's Word and the Lord's own word on the matter of his return, but it is also denied if people reject a godly life-style and live immorally.

who bought them is a phrase that has caused considerable discussion. At face value its meaning seems obvious. These people are denying the very (slave) Master who purchased them for himself. The phrase is a simple and moving qualification of who the Master is. He is the one who went out of his way to purchase these people for himself and now they are even denying him. What a sad reflection on the depth of their sin and of their rejection of his Lordship!

However, an important theological question is raised by this statement. If the 'buying' refers, as seems most natural, to Jesus' sacrificial death on the cross through which he 'purchased men for God from every tribe and language and people and nation' (Revelation 5:9), then it would appear some have been saved only to lose their salvation later. The problem with saying this, however, is that we need to balance Scripture with Scripture where there is ample evidence that, in fact, those who are saved by the grace of Christ are indeed finally saved. So certain is this that the apostle Paul can speak of those who are saved by grace as already being seated 'with him in the heavenly realms in Christ Jesus' (see the whole of Ephesians 2:1-10). Jesus himself also says clearly, 'I give [my sheep] eternal life, and they shall never perish; no-one can snatch them out of my hand. My Father, who has given them to me, is greater than all; no-one can snatch them out of my Father's hand' (John 10:28-29).[16]

Perhaps the best explanation of what is actually happening here in 2 Peter is that these false teachers were never truly 'saved' though they were claiming to have committed

---

16. Many other passages teach clearly the possibility of real Christian assurance of eternal life and the impossibility of final damnation for those who 'have been saved' (note past tense). The basis of this teaching is, of course, that salvation is of grace from the God who elects and calls his people to himself and, in Peter's own words, continues to provide all that is necessary to continue in that faith to the end. As Paul said in Philippians 1:6: 'being confident of this, that he who began a good work in you will carry it on to completion until the day of Christ Jesus.' See also Romans 8:33-39.

themselves to the Lord who redeems his people. God's people do not 'bring swift destruction on themselves'! Dr Kistemaker in his commentary puts it well: 'If we look at [these words] in the light of the broader context, we discover a clue. We notice that at one time these false teachers professed the name of Christ, for they said that they knew him and the way of righteousness (2:20-21). They made it known that Jesus had bought them, but they eventually rejected Christ and left the Christian community. As John writes, "They went out from us, but they did not really belong to us" (1 John 2:19) ... Hence their denial of Christ showed that they were not redeemed.'[17]

b) They attract others (verse 2)

One way or another, the awful seriousness of the situation is made clear. These people are abusing the wonderful grace of the Lord Jesus Christ and denying his Lordship. In spite of this, Peter insists that, **Many will follow their shameful ways and will bring the way of truth into disrepute** (verse 2). Herein lies one of the greatest tragedies faced by the Christian church. There were, are and always will be people who will follow these false teachers in their **shameful ways**. There are always people around who are gullible and swept along by kind words or powerful leadership, but there are others who are always on the look out for anything that is new or

---

17. Simon J. Kistemaker, *Peter and Jude* (Baker, 1987), p. 282. Another of the many explanations of this verse is offered by Wayne Grudem, *Systematic Theology* (IVP, 1994), p. 600. He suggests that Peter is drawing on Deuteronomy 32:6. There Moses is referring to the Father 'buying' the rebellious Israelites from Egypt. Any Jew would have considered himself to have been 'bought' out of (redeemed from) Egypt by God. Thus, he believes, Peter's concern for the false teachers is that 'they were rebellious Jewish people (or church attenders in the same position as the rebellious Jews) who were rightly owned by God because they had been brought out of the land of Egypt (or their forefathers had), but they were ungrateful to him. 'Christ's specific redemptive work on the cross is not in view in this verse.'

might give them a slightly different so-called 'spiritual' experience.

shameful ways here may simply mean that everything taught by the people leads away from **the way of truth** and that is always shameful. It is more likely that it refers to immorality that so often accompanies those who teach falsely and lead away from the truth.

The way of truth recalls Peter's emphasis on the revealed truth of the apostolic gospel in Chapter 1. It is the way of Christ as Lord and Master, following his teaching, trusting and believing in him, seeking to obey him and, specially in this context, looking for his Second Coming.[18] Christianity itself had become known as 'the Way' (Acts 9:2), but here Peter may well have in mind Psalm 119:29-30 where the Psalmist prays to be kept from 'deceitful ways' and talks of having 'chosen the way of truth', by which he means he has 'set his heart on God's laws'.

Special Lessons for Today

Three issues ought to be given great priority as today's teachers seek to uphold the same biblical truth of the gospel message against those who want to **secretly introduce destructive heresies**.

First, it should be noted that there is a difference between slight variations of teachings and 'destructive' variants. Peter is not denying the right of Christians to disagree over matters of interpretation. We are not infallible interpreters of the

---

18. In spite of the close associations with Jude in this section of 2 Peter, verse 2 contains an indication that their audiences were different. At this stage there is no mention by Peter of the detail of their immorality and he does not talk of the grace of God being changed into a licence for immorality. Richard Bauckham (*Jude, 2 Peter*, Word Biblical Commentaries, Word Books, 1983, p. 241) plausibly suggests that in Jude the problem is 'an antinomian interpretation of grace', while Peter is concerned with those who, denying future judgment, had slipped back 'into pagan ways'. See my commentary on Jude in this volume.

Word, rather we have an infallible Word of God that fallible Christians are called upon to interpret and apply. We will no doubt get things wrong. The guide, however, for deciding what is right is to be Scripture itself. The fallible interpreter must not think, as many commentators seem to, that he or she is the infallible one. There must be a humility before the Word of God and a desire to seek help in understanding from those who show real evidence of the work of God in their lives. This could be developed at length, but the point is clear. There is a crying need in the church today to see what fundamentally challenges the truth of Scripture and to see it as *false*.

Secondly, there is a general naiveté around among many Christians that somehow false teachers will be easily recognised. Peter is as adamant as Jude in Jude 4, that these people do not announce themselves as impostors! It may sound almost silly, but if they did they would quickly get thrown out of most churches. Nevertheless, people are all too easily conned by those who have an appearance of godliness. Perhaps they appear loving and caring. Maybe they proclaim what they call their 'spiritual gifts' for all to see. Maybe they have a way with words. But one way or another they worm their way into the congregation and **secretly introduce** falsehood. It is time for the church to wake up again. There is no doubt that many sections of the church have been and are being wooed away from biblical truth. Sadly this truth is often seen as a bit too 'heavy' or dictatorial among people and even churches that at best lack godliness and at worst thoroughly ignore God's Word.

Thirdly, we need to be aware that new spiritualities and sects are rearing their heads every few weeks in our day and age. Some are obviously to be rejected. Others, like those Peter deals with, are more 'secretly introduced'. They seem fair enough. They have attractive qualities about them and

are perhaps close enough to orthodox biblical faith that people
do not immediately see the problem with them. It is interesting
that many false teachings are once again surfacing about the
return of Christ, specially as we cross from the second to the
third millennium. Some are saying that they know when he
will return. Others go the opposite way altogether and, like
Peter's opponents, suggest that the whole idea of a bodily
return of Christ is a nonsense. Some suggest that any future
is to be understood in entirely 'spiritual' terms by which they
mean something almost pantheistic with a merging of the
human and divine. Others admit to a Second Coming but
deny judgment. Indeed this latter position is held by some in
almost all the major denominations of the Christian church
around the world. Closely linked to this is the teaching
espoused by many 'Christian' teachers that there are many
ways that lead to God, even if the way of Jesus is the best.
When these teachings are carefully put in terms of the 'love'
of God for his people and the 'non-judgmental Jesus who
loves everyone', it is fairly easy to see how many will follow
these lies. They do not immediately appear to people as error.
In a world where any proposition concerning absolute truth
is scorned, then it becomes clear that false teaching in the
church may well find a fertile ground in which to flourish.
Let's make sure we learn from Peter for today!

c) They are greedy (verse 3)

**In their greed these teachers will exploit you with stories they
have made up. Their condemnation has long been hanging
over them, and their destruction has not been sleeping** (verse 3).

It appears from 1:16 that the false teachers had accused Peter
and the apostles of following **cleverly invented stories**
(myths). The reality is the opposite. These teachers have
themselves exploited people, and drawn them from the truth

with stories they have made up. No doubt they had asked those who followed them for financial support in their 'ministries', hence what Peter calls their **greed**. This is a matter that he addresses again in verses 15-16 where he uses Balaam as an example of one who was greedy.

Peter is intent on letting his readers know that the very people who deny the Second Coming and judgment of Christ and who exploit other Christians will indeed be judged when Christ returns. In the second half of verse 3, which both completes the thought of the first couple of verses and links into what follows, Peter makes the point again: **Their condemnation has long been hanging over them**. This will not be a pleasant message for those who are still scornfully asking 'Where is this "coming" he promised?' (3:4). Great force is added to the point as Peter says the same thing again in the second half of the sentence but using different words, **and their destruction has not been sleeping**.

Both condemnation and destruction are somewhat personalised here by Peter. The idea is that the one has not been 'idle' and the other is not 'sleeping'! The picture is vivid that judgment will appear as an active force and it is on its way, **long** prophesied. Peter has already argued that the Old Testament prophets foretold the coming of Christ and the final judgment, but in the verses that follow he also looks at Old Testament examples of God's judgment and sees in them a foretelling of the final judgment of God.

Sometimes as we see false teachers at work, we are tempted to think that they cannot be all that bad, specially if they are very nice people and talk of God and his love. It is important to remember that they will face the wrath of God on the final day of judgment and that their doom has been prophesied for many, many generations. What do these people have to do with the **way of truth**? Nothing!

So in these first three verses Peter goes on the offensive

against false teachers. First, he says that their presence among
God's people is a fact. They were there in the past and they
will always seek to influence biblical Christians with their
shameful ways in a bid to lead them away from the way of
truth. Secondly, Peter shows that these teachers will act in a
secretive way in introducing their lies. In practice they will
deny the sovereign Lord. However, God's people can be
encouraged, for these heretics, in spite of their denial of
Christ's return and the final judgment, will indeed be judged.
The teachers will be recognisable both by their denial of the
Lord in their way of life, and by their greed. They will make
up stories to support their views. But God is sovereign and it
must be remembered that *their destruction has not been
sleeping*!

d) They will be condemned, *but* God protects the righteous (verses 4-10)

Peter has already maintained (1:19-21) that the Scriptures
are the word of God, revealed to the prophets by his Spirit,
and are therefore utterly to be relied upon. So it is to these
that Peter now turns to draw out two vital lessons for the
church of all ages.

First, he wants to demonstrate that the fate of false teachers
is certain. But secondly, he also wants God's people to know
that God protects the righteous. In these verses these two
themes are intertwined and we shall look at them separately.
But before that we pause in order briefly to discuss the
relationship between what follows in 2 Peter 2 and the epistle
of Jude.

Relationship to Jude

It is in this section and the rest of chapter 2 that we see
the clearest overlap between 2 Peter and Jude. Both
Peter and Jude refer to angels being judged (verse 4;

Jude 6), to Sodom and Gomorrah (verse 6; Jude 7) and
to Balaam (verse 15; Jude 11). Both have similar
descriptions of the false teachers and use similar
metaphors to describe their depravity.

However, while admitting the close similarities
between this part of 2 Peter and Jude, it is very important
that we do not simply believe we have understood 2
Peter 2 if we have understood Jude, or vice versa. The
differences between the two passages and the
differences of subject matter of the epistles as a whole
should alert us to the fact that, while both are making
some similar points, each tackles important concerns
not dealt with by the other. It is surely because of this,
of course, that under God's providence we have both
books as Scripture.

As to the differences, it is specially to be noted that,
in what follows, Peter refers to Noah and to Lot, while
Jude does not. Jude goes into detail about the angels
and refers to the archangel Michael and to the
intertestamental book of Enoch, which Peter does not.
Jude also mentions the judgments of Cain and Korah,
both missing in 2 Peter. Even where the same incidents
are mentioned, different vocabulary is often, but not
always used. Peter cites his examples in chronological
order, Jude does not. While both are intent on
emphasising God's judgment, we shall see that Peter
also emphasises from the examples of Noah and Lot,
the salvation of those who are faithful.

As indicated in the Introduction, I do not believe it
is possible to conclude on the basis of the evidence either
that Jude wrote first and used Peter or that Peter wrote
first and was then picked up by Jude. It is at least
possible that they knew each other and wrote around
the same time, though this would simply be conjecture.

What is known is that some intertestamental literature draws together various examples of judgment and uses them in teaching about the need for righteousness. Moreover we know that all the examples used also appear in teaching for righteousness in Scripture, so it is more than likely that early Christianity had learned from Jewish teaching to put these accounts of judgment together.

So we return to Peter's three illustrations from the Old Testament. The sentence structure is very complicated here. In fact, in the Greek, there is a single sentence running from the start of verse 4 through to the middle of verse 10 all introduced by a single 'if' at the start! The New International Version helps considerably by introducing not only verse 4 with the word 'if' but also verses 5, 6, 7, and 9 and starting a new sentence with verse 10.

However, it is in verse 9 that we see what Peter wants us to conclude from his examples: **if this is so, then the Lord knows how to rescue godly men from trials and to hold the unrighteous for the day of judgment, while continuing their punishment**. Two deductions from the Scriptures must be held together. Throughout trials and temptations the righteous will be preserved and rescued, as were Noah and Lot; but the unrighteous will experience judgment while themselves being preserved by God for final judgment. This, then, is the conclusion of this section of the epistle and needs to be borne in mind as the specific examples Peter employs are now examined in more detail.

1) Examples of judgment
Peter continues to build his case against the false teachers who are denying Christ's return and final judgment and who are living lives of greed and immorality. **For if God did not spare angels when they sinned, but sent them to hell, putting them**

into gloomy dungeons to be held for judgment (verse 4).

This first illustration is likely to appear thoroughly obscure to the modern reader. The Old Testament does not explicitly refer to God judging the angels. However, there are passages in the Bible as a whole that some take as referring to the judgment of angels and specially Satan. For example, in Revelation 12:7-9 the apostle John saw in his vision a war between Michael and his angels and the dragon (Satan) and his angels, in which Satan was hurled to the earth.[19] When all this happened is not really clear in Scripture but, presumably, it was prior to Satan's appearance in the Garden of Eden and his temptation of Eve.

Others see a reference to Satan's fall and perhaps the fall of his angels in Isaiah 14:9-17 and in Ezekiel 28:11-19. While it is possible that the reference is to the same events as recounted in Revelation 12, that is far from clear. These latter two texts are more likely to refer directly to judgments on particular kings. Nevertheless, the vivid imagery and hyperbole used in the description may be based upon ideas of the fall of Satan. We cannot be certain.

The view adopted here, in common with most modern commentators, is that Peter is most likely drawing upon an understanding of Genesis 6:1-4. In the biblical text this is a lead-in to the account of the judgment of the flood which Peter picks up in verse 5. It talks of how the numbers of people on earth were growing rapidly and how their sin continued (Gen. 6:1). Part of God's judgment was to be a limitation on the length of their lives to 120 years (6:3). Most of this is straightforward enough, but we also read: 'the sons of God saw that the daughters of men were beautiful, and they married any of them they chose' (verse 2), and (verse 4): 'The Nephilim were on the earth in those days – and also afterwards – when

---

19. This bears some similarity to Jesus' comment in Luke 10:18 where he said 'saw Satan fall like lightning from heaven'.

the sons of God went to the daughters of men and had children
by them. They were the heroes of old, men of renown.'

This difficult and somewhat obscure text in Genesis was
taken in inter-testamental Jewish teachings (specially in the
Book of Enoch[20]) to refer to fallen angels who had unlawful
sexual intercourse with women. In other words the phrase
'sons of God' is taken to refer to angels. These angels were
then subject to the judgment of God who did not destroy
them but has kept them 'in chains' under the earth for the
final judgment day when they will be banished to eternal
fire. The account in the book of Enoch elaborates on this in
all sorts of far-fetched detail, giving names to the leaders of
the angels and suggesting that these angels helped teach
human beings about even greater depths of sin.

The problem for us is that it is not at all clear that Genesis
6 is talking about angels at all. Certainly this has long been a
matter of debate among Christian scholars. Very early
Christian writers understood it in the way these
intertestamental Jewish texts did but, later, as people studied
the passage more closely many came to believe, as most do
today, that 'sons of God' was more likely a reference to the
men who were in the world at the time.[21]

In the passage in Jude where this same example is
employed, the book of Enoch is explicitly quoted. It therefore
remains likely that, while not wanting to refer his readers
directly, as Jude does, to a book they had probably never
seen, Peter does indeed have Genesis 6 in mind as he speaks
of God's judgment on the angels for their sin.

If this is so, then a couple more things need to be said.

---

20. Enoch is directly quoted in Jude who also uses this example. Bauckham
(*Jude, 2 Peter*, p. 248) assumes that Peter is indirectly using Enoch because
he is here dependent upon Jude who explicitly mentions Enoch. However,
we have said above that we do not consider the case proven that Peter
depended on Jude.

21. For discussion on Jude's use of Enoch, see my comments on pp. 231-234.

First, given the context of Peter's reciting examples from history, these happenings with the angels must also be treated as history. It seems a nonsense to assume that, though references to Noah and Lot are taken as historical, this one is a mere mythical illustration. In other words, whatever Peter's source for what he says here about the angels who sinned and their judgment, we may assume that the incident is historical and that it is true as God's word and properly interpreted by the apostle as he is guided by the Holy Spirit to write.

Second, and most importantly, it is vital as we interpret God's word in Scripture that, just as we should not take away from that word, so we should not add to that word. The fact of the matter is that, apart from serving as an example from which we must learn, what happened to angels and God's subsequent judgment of them is not elaborated upon in Scripture and is not really the business of human beings!

Speculation on such matters is once again leading the church away from the substance of the gospel into myths and fantasies. This is a feature of much 'New Age' teaching and it has infiltrated its way back into the church with all sorts of fantastical claims about angels and their work among us. Peter lived in a day when such myths abounded, we could do well to learn from him. He says little here but simply uses the historical judgment of angels who sinned as a reminder to God's people for all time that God does indeed judge sin and will therefore judge again.

So we return to verse 4. **For if God did not spare angels when they sinned, but sent them to hell, putting them into gloomy dungeons[22] to be held for judgment ...** Peter emphasises two points as he continues to describe the judgment of the angels. The first is that they have been **sent**

22. As the New International Version footnote shows, some manuscripts replace 'dungeons' with 'chains of darkness'. In the roughly parallel passage of Jude 6 the word used is 'chains'. The Greek words involved are very similar indeed (*sirois* – 'pits', hence dungeons; *seirais* – 'chains'; though it

to hell. The word Peter uses here is connected to the Greek mythological location known as Tartarus. Of course, Peter is by no means affirming a belief in the Greek myths in which Tartarus is the place of punishment in the depths of the underworld. He is simply using a word that would have been recognised in the culture of the day as referring to a place of judgment. Just as people today will often use the word 'hell' to describe a difficult period in their lives without any reference back to the biblical place of eternal punishment, so Peter was able to use the word 'Tartarus' to describe a place of judgment but without all the Greek mythological baggage attached. The angels have been judged.

However, the second point Peter is making is that the *final* judgment has yet to come. The angels are being **held for judgment**. Jude talks of them being *kept* for judgment just as the righteous are being *kept* for salvation. The false teachers Peter is fighting are saying that there is no judgment to come. Peter argues from this example that there *is* a final judgment and that the fallen angels are evidence of that event for they yet await their final destiny. In this sense we need to realise also that 'hell' is not an ideal translation for us today. Normally in biblical terms we use the word 'hell' to describe the place of permanent and eternal judgment, the place to which people will be consigned at the return of Christ if they have refused to acknowledge him as Lord and Saviour. Here Peter is clearly describing a temporary confinement or limitation upon the fallen angels, pending that final judgment that has yet to come.

if he did not spare the ancient world when he brought the flood on its ungodly people (verse 5) continues Peter's theme of judgment. (We shall return to the second half of

---

is worth noting that Jude uses a different Greek word for 'chains'). In fact, whichever way this word is read really makes no difference to the meaning, which is that the angels are being held for final judgment.

this verse shortly.) This time his reference is back to God's judgment at the time of the Flood which is recounted in Genesis 6:5-7:24. 'Noah's flood' as it has become known in modern English is proverbial for God's judgment as much as the next example in verse 6 where we read: **if he condemned the cities of Sodom and Gomorrah by burning them to ashes, and made them an example of what is going to happen to the ungodly ...**

There are no two more evocative images of the horror of divine judgment than the Flood and the destruction of the cities of Sodom and Gomorrah (Genesis 19). And this is precisely why Peter uses them both as examples. His main points that he made with the judgment of the angels are both again to be seen here but now the judgment concerns *people*. These judgments which happened in history demonstrate that God has judged and will judge the ungodly. Yet even these fearful judgments are but **an example of what is going to happen to the ungodly** (verse 6) at the return of Christ.

The emphasis in both examples is first and foremost on the *extent* of the judgment. It is *all* the ungodly who are judged. Indeed at the time of the flood only eight people were saved, **Noah ... and seven others**.[23] In the case of Sodom and Gomorrah it was even fewer for only Lot, his wife and his two daughters were saved, and even then his wife eventually was judged (Genesis 19:15-16, 26).

The staggering thing to remember here is that both Noah and Lot had tried to persuade others of the danger of such ungodliness and yet none had taken any notice at all. The fact of the matter is that the depth of the depravity of sin takes over people so entirely that they cannot see righteousness for what it is, nor hear about it, nor begin to understand it. These two examples are graphic illustrations of the apostle Paul's description of the way the ungodly

23. See also 1 Peter 3:20.

deliberately suppress 'the truth of their wickedness' and so exchange 'the truth of God for a lie' (Romans 1:18-25).

Both examples were widely used in Jewish writings as warnings. But as Peter refers to them he may well have been specially recalling the teaching of the Lord on the matter of his return as the 'Son of Man' and the final judgment 'day' in Luke 17:26-30. There Jesus himself referred to both the Flood and Sodom[24] and Gomorrah.

The false teachers ought to have known from history that God judges the ungodly and then holds them for the final day of judgment. This is Peter's direct application in verse 9: **if this is so, then the Lord knows how to ... hold the unrighteous for the day of judgment....** The warnings are dire and must be heeded. Christ will return and judge. The judgment of angels in the past, of the ungodly at the time of the Flood, and in the cities of Sodom and Gomorrah are all to be seen as warnings and even foretastes of the final judgment day and the future experience of all who are unrighteous. As none of the ungodly survived the Flood or the fire of Sodom and Gomorrah, so none will survive the return of Christ but will rather be judged to eternal hell.

while continuing their punishment reminds us again that men and women should be aware of what will happen when God finally acts in judgment. The phrase is reminiscent of Romans 1:24 where we read that those who are caught up in the sin of moral degradation God gives over to 'the sinful desires of their hearts'. Even during this life people find themselves experiencing a foretaste of what will come as God brings judgment that continues even while people are kept for the final judgment day.

---

24. Sodom is used as a warning of further judgment on a number of other occasions in Scripture, e.g. Isaiah 3:9; 13:19; Jeremiah 23:14; 49:18. In Lamentations 4:6 the judgment on Sodom is used to help explain what God was then doing to Jerusalem! Also see Amos 4:11. See also Jesus' teaching in Matthew 10:15.

2) Examples of salvation

So fearful are these judgments that there is a real danger of
the righteous wondering about their own salvation. Perhaps
they too may get caught up in the conflagration. What will
happen to those who 'have received a faith as precious as'
Peter's? Are they in danger? Peter's teaching here is vital
and it indicates just why these two particular judgments of
the Flood and of Sodom and Gomorrah came to be regarded
as 'types' of the great judgment yet to come. In both cases
the 'righteous', those who worshipped the Lord, were saved.
It is this fact that forms Peter's second main point in verse 5
and then in verses 7 and 8. And it is this fact that should give
great encouragement to the Lord's people who continue to
live as aliens and strangers in an ungodly world.

In verse 5, having spoken of judgment, Peter adds: **but
protected Noah, a preacher of righteousness, and seven
others**. Here is amazing encouragement for believers. Here
is that wonderful demonstration of God's grace in the midst
of dealing with the most sinful people. God **protected Noah**.

One of the most comforting doctrines in Scripture is that
once we belong to God, once we have been called to be his
and received his saving and forgiving grace in our lives, then
we are held secure by him. Jesus himself explicitly teaches
this in John 10:27-29: 'My sheep listen to my voice; I know
them, and they follow me. I give them eternal life, and they
shall never perish; no one can snatch them out of my hand.
My Father, who has given them to me, is greater than all; no
one can snatch them out of my Father's hand. I and the Father
are one.'[25] The apostle Paul re-affirms this great doctrine of
grace on many occasions. Perhaps Philippians 1:6 best sums
up the link that Peter also makes between God's preserving
work and surviving the day of Christ's return: 'being
confident of this, that he who began a good work in you will

---

25. In one way or another most of the writers of Scripture affirm this teaching.

carry it on to completion until the day of Christ Jesus.'

Peter's comment that Noah was **a preacher of right-eousness** is worthy of note. We have no record of Noah 'preaching' in Genesis, but what we do read is that 'Noah was a righteous man, blameless among the people of his time, and he walked with God'. Peter is insisting that the 'ungodly' are judged and will be judged. Noah was truly 'godly'. Godliness and ungodliness have to do with the way people are in their life and thought and speech. Either they live righteously, that is, in accordance with the will and purposes of God, or else they do not and are to be classed as 'ungodly'. What is so easily forgotten is that we are all able to see godliness or ungodliness in each other's lives. Noah 'preached' no doubt with his speech as he pleaded with people to repent or to join him in the ark, but the Bible does not tell us of that. Rather we have every indication that Noah 'preached' through his life-style and the way he continued to obey the Lord in the midst of ungodly people. This is the idea picked up in Hebrews 11:7 where Noah is commended for his faith: 'By his faith [Noah] condemned the world and became heir of the righteousness that comes by faith.' His very actions of obedience served further to condemn those around.

We should take the matter of 'preaching' through our way of life, our obedience and day to day living for the Lord very seriously. So often Christians do not really stand out from the crowd and so the appeal for righteousness is rarely seen or heard.

Peter continues to describe God's protection of the right-eous in verses 7 and 8: **and if he rescued Lot, a righteous man, who was distressed by the filthy lives of lawless men (for that righteous man, living among them day after day, was tormented in his righteous soul by the lawless deeds he saw and heard).**

Lot lived in Sodom (Genesis 18–19), one of the cities of the Jordan valley. God graciously **rescued** him from the devastating judgment he brought upon the city and its people as a result of their sin. Though these cities would have been little more than market towns by today's standard, they nevertheless exhibited a life-style common in today's larger cities. Here was a whole culture that exhibited the depravity of men and women. The people were **lawless**. They were quite the opposite of Lot who was **righteous**. They led **filthy lives**, which speaks of their sexual depravity.[26]

Lot **was tormented in his righteous soul by the lawless deeds he saw and heard**. At first this may seem strange to us who know from the narrative of Genesis 18–19 that Lot seemed very reluctant to leave Sodom. After all, it was he who had chosen to live in that area (Genesis 13:10-13). Commentators spend much time discussing why Lot should be regarded as 'righteous'. The most likely answer lies in a combination of two facts. The first is that in Genesis 18:23 Abraham intercedes on behalf of the 'righteous' who may be living in Sodom and Gomorrah. Since Lot is eventually delivered as an answer to that prayer, it is a legitimate deduction to assume that Lot was 'righteous'. However, something deeper than that was going on. As a member of Abraham's extended family, Lot was being protected by God as a member of the covenant family, the 'righteous'. Lot's rescue from Sodom in answer to Abraham's prayer is not only the rescue of a 'righteous' man but a clear keeping of covenant promises to Abraham.

Nevertheless, the closest the text of Genesis gets to showing Lot as **distressed** and **tormented** is when the men of the city call upon him to send out his two visitors so they

---

26. See a fuller description of this sort of pagan life in 1 Peter 4:3 where the same word in Greek is translated in the New International Version as 'debauchery'.

can be sexually used (Genesis 19:5). Lot's response to such wicked behaviour (19:6) is genuine torment and horror. Lot may not have always been wise in choosing where to live or which friends to have, but he was indeed concerned at serious evil and was rescued by the Lord from destruction.

And so we return to verse 9 – **if this** [i.e. the protecting of Noah and Lot and the judgment of the angels, the Flood and the burning of Sodom and Gomorrah] **is so, then the Lord knows how to rescue godly men from trials and to hold the unrighteous for the day of judgment while continuing their punishment**. We have seen how God rescued these godly men from **trials**. **Trials** here has to do with what godly people experience as they live in this fallen world. In 1 Peter 1:6 Peter has also talked of God's protection of his people in this age and continues: 'In this you greatly rejoice, though now for a little while you may have had to suffer grief in all kinds of trials.'

We have also seen how God has judged the ungodly. Once again Peter stresses that their final judgment is certain and such people are currently being held **for the day of judgment**. We often fail to realise that as the ungodly of this world continue in their way of sin and evil they are actually being *held* by God for that final judgment. More than this, Peter is teaching that what they are experiencing even now is a continuing punishment. This reminds us of Romans 1:24-32 where we are told 'God gave them [evil people] over in the sinful desires of their hearts to sexual immorality ... and received in themselves the due penalty ...'. It is a common thought in Scripture that people receive *now* in their lives a foretaste of the judgment to come. Peter has already pointed to this in 2 Peter 2:3: **their judgment has long been hanging over them** – prophesied for the future, certainly, but surely it is more than that. These people have pointers in their normal lives, given by God, which indicate that they are already being judged as they are held by God for that final day.

So the Christians Peter writes to are encouraged. They are reminded that God will always keep and protect and rescue them in the midst of a world that is deeply sinful and evil, a world in which godliness is despised and where Christians will be subjected to all sorts of trials. But they are also reminded that those who are evil and cause great suffering to Christians are already experiencing something of God's judgment while awaiting the certainty of final judgment at the return of Christ. It is of course the greatest irony that the very event they are suggesting will never happen is the event that will bring about their final and complete condemnation.

Special Lessons for Today

First, we need to be able to recognise ungodliness for what it is. The distinctiveness of our Christian lives will lead to trials and sufferings in this world and this will be uncomfortable. But how clearly are we standing for righteousness? It is all too easy to be too tolerant of ungodliness. It may bring a rather more peaceful life, but it is not how God wants us to be. As Peter put it in his first epistle, God does expect us to be and to feel like 'aliens and strangers in the world' (1 Peter 2:11).

Secondly, we need to recover a conviction in the modern church of the certainty of judgment on the final day. Just as the false teachers of Peter's day denied Christ's Second Coming and the finality of judgment on that day, so we are surrounded in our generation by people saying similar things. As we look at this evil world with all its sin, we must live and work in it while remembering that its days are limited. The day is coming that **will bring about the destruction of the heavens by fire and the elements will melt in the heat** (2 Peter 3:12). While we preach righteousness, like Noah, through our lives and with our lips, let us do so with an urgency that is well aware of what the future holds for those who do not repent.

Thirdly, we need to find real comfort and joy in the verses we have read. God has made covenant promises to all who have faith in him and trust in Christ and he will keep these as faithfully as he kept them with Noah and Lot. The righteous are people who belong to God, and all who do belong to him will be protected by him. This is the encouragement of these verses. Sometimes the trials of this world and the evil with which we are surrounded seems rather over-powering. Many Christians these days seem so pessimistic about life and the world in which we live. But we are God's people through faith in Jesus Christ, and this is God's world and he remains sovereign. We look forward to that sovereignty, of which we see evidence even today in our own lives, being made manifest to the whole world. We look forward too to that great day of Christ's return and to the time when there will be a **new heaven and a new earth, the home of righteousness** (2 Peter 3:13).

The first part of verse 10 summarises this part of Peter's writing: the false teachers he and his readers face will most certainly be condemned. **This is especially true of those who follow the corrupt desire of the sinful nature and despise authority**. Peter lays the greater emphasis on the pending judgment for those who are immoral, indulging, as the Greek puts it, the *polluting lust of the flesh*. He is comparing the people Lot faced and whom Noah faced with people of his day. Such a comparison is easy enough to make with the modern age as well.

What is meant by despising authority is not altogether clear. The word translated **authority** is *kuriotetos*. The next part of verse 10 and into verse 11 talks of angels. So it is possible to take this despising of authority to refer to despising angelic beings (see a somewhat similar use of the word in Ephesians 1:21). In a roughly parallel sentence in Jude 8, however, the word refers to despising the authority of the Lord. And it is perhaps better to take it this way here too. This would then be recalling 2:1 where they deny the sovereign Lord. The word *kuriotetos* really means 'lordship', in this case probably the Lordship of God himself. Hand in hand with following the lusts of the flesh goes a despising of the authority of the Lord himself. Such people are lawless (verse 7).

5. Recognise false prophets and teachers (2:10b-22)

The second part of verse 10 leads into a more detailed description of the sin and lawlessness of these false teachers. Peter wants his readers to recognise who these evil leaders are and carefully to apply what he is saying to their own church situation.

a) They are blasphemous hedonists (verses 10b-16)

Bold and arrogant, these men are not afraid to slander celestial beings. It is often the case that false teachers are 'full of it'. They proclaim with pride that what they are teaching is the only right understanding of things. They put down orthodox teaching with great arrogance. Peter talks about their slander of angels.[27] Whether he has in mind their slander of good angels (as Jude 8 does), or of evil angels, matters little here. But the next verse helps us understand a little more of Peter's point.

yet even angels, although they are stronger and more powerful, do not bring slanderous accusations against such beings in the presence of the Lord (verse 11). Peter now expands on his view that the false teachers can be recognised by their slanderous arrogance. In slandering angels these evil men are doing something that they are not entitled

---

27. In spite of some suggestions to the contrary, the word *doxas* here surely refers to angels rather than ecclesiastical or civil authorities, as some from time to time have suggested. This alone makes good sense of verse 11 which uses the angels as an example.

to do. God's dealings with angels are for him alone and are not for us to interfere with.

The background event that Peter has in mind, where angels did not do what these men are doing, is obscure. It is likely he had in mind the story referred to explicitly in Jude 9. The parallels between 2 Peter 2:11-12 and Jude 9-10 are helpful, although we need to remember that Peter may not have exactly the same things in mind. For example, Peter refers to 'angels' (plural) rather than to one (Michael), and his final application is somewhat different. Nevertheless, Jude refers to the archangel Michael himself not daring to bring an accusation against the devil but rather saying 'The Lord rebuke you!'[28] And this is similar to the point Peter is making. It was vital for his readers to understand that, in slandering the angels, the false teachers were doing something that was utterly unacceptable and seriously arrogant and wicked. The fact that Peter makes no reference to the detail or the specifics we have in Jude, should make us pause to reflect that such information was not in fact important to Peter. Rather the lesson about arrogance and boldness in matters over which they had no competence or knowledge was what needed to be heeded. Even though the angels were **stronger and more powerful** than those they were accusing, they did not enter an area of authority that clearly belonged to God. And this is just the matter he points to in the first sentence of verse 12.

But these men blaspheme in matters they do not understand. They make pronouncements that deny the Lord and his truth, and they arrogantly claim to have the truth in areas which they actually do not understand at all. The area of life they fail to comprehend no doubt has to do with spiritual understanding of matters of the Lord and his will for his people and for this world. In fact, **they are like brute beasts,**

---

28. See Appendix: Michael, an accusation and the dispute over the body of Moses.

creatures of instinct, born only to be caught and destroyed, and like beasts they too will perish (verse 12).

The comparison of the false teachers and prophets with brute beasts is dramatic. Brute beasts do not have spiritual understanding. They do not understand the will of the Lord for his people, or the place of angels, or the need for behaviour that is godly. They do not understand about judgment and salvation or about sexual immorality and arrogance. Rather they simply live according to their natural instincts. This is what the false teachers are like, says Peter. His indictment is damning and extremely pointed.

Such people are heading for death and destruction. However, it is worth noting that the New International Version translation, **and like beasts they too will perish**, is a somewhat free translation of a rather difficult Greek sentence. As we have seen, the meaning is ultimately clear enough. These leaders will be destroyed. But the Greek says something like, *will themselves be destroyed in their destruction*. The repetition of 'destroyed' and 'destruction' is clearly emphatic. Perhaps Peter is thinking of the fact that beasts are reared with a view to their being killed in sacrifice or for eating, and so these evil teachers know their destruction will be as final and as sudden as that experienced by the animals with whom they have just been compared.

Peter's emphasis on the retribution that God will bring about continues in verse 13.[29] **They will be paid back with harm for the harm they have done** (verse 13). These people have brought harm to God's people and so will be paid back with harm. The Greek makes another play on words which is not really possible to translate, but may approximately be translated as, 'they will be wronged as a wage for the wrong they have done'. Of course Peter is not in any way attributing

29. The New International Version puts a paragraph division before verse 13, but this is not necessary.

wrong to God in judging them, he is simply saying that they will receive the just recompense for their evil.

Special Lessons for Today

While the verses we have just looked at can be applied in many different ways, two points are specially worthy of note for Christians living today. First, Peter does not beat around the bush in the way he speaks of these false teachers. In an age when tolerance is virtually the new religion, and anything that seems to the world to lack tolerance is regarded as 'fundamentalism' (the new 'dirty word' of the post-modern age), we need to hear how an apostle regarded such people. Tolerance of such rampant evil and blasphemy is simply unacceptable. We need to make sure that we not only speak of heresy and blasphemy for what it is, but also that we recognise in our minds and attitudes to such people that their heresies really will lead to damnation and are utterly evil and need to be contradicted.

Secondly, we often lose sight of the inherent *justice* of God even in his judgment. Already in this epistle we have seen how God's judgment in effect gives people what they have been asking for. The expression 'you are asking for it' takes on a real significance when we look at how God deals with people. Sinful people acting like animals will be treated like animals. People who harm others will find harm coming on them. Those who dare to pronounce blasphemy and slander against things they do not even understand will find God judging them as they would have judged others.

> **Their idea of pleasure is to carouse in broad daylight. They are blots and blemishes, revelling in their pleasures while they feast with you** (verse 13).

Having discussed in greater detail the sin of these false teachers and their impending judgment, Peter returns to describe another aspect of their wickedness. They will also be noted for their carousing, revelling and feasting. This paints a picture of self-indulgence and sexual impropriety that is entirely unacceptable among God's people. Instead of pleasure in worship and in caring for each other and reaching out to others with the gospel of Christ, these people seem to exist only for themselves and have become so influenced by the thinking of the world that they have entirely forgotten the biblical call to holiness.

Peter will call true believers back to holiness and godliness in 3:11-12 as he reminds them again of 'the day of God' when destruction and judgment will come. There he asks them to **make every effort to be found spotless and blameless** on that final day. These words are the exact opposite of blots and blemishes which we have here in 2:13. Spotlessness recalls the requirement in Leviticus for an offering to be spotless (Leviticus 1:3). These people were certainly not living up to the standards and demands expected of God's people which the apostle Paul so aptly summarised in Romans 12:1: 'offer your bodies as living sacrifices, holy and pleasing to God – this is your spiritual act of worship'.

Whether Peter has in mind a **feasting** related to a full meal that accompanied the Lord's Supper is unclear. Nevertheless, feasting often carried with it a level of sexual indulgence and of drunkenness which Christians should have nothing to do with. Even the pagans would have reserved such activity for the evenings and night time, while these people were indulging themselves **in broad daylight**. As we might say today, 'they had no shame'! So far removed were their teachings and life-style from the traditional biblical teachings that Christians should be a *holy* people unto God, that they no longer even seemed to think that such behaviour might be *sin*.

With eyes full of adultery, they never stop sinning;

they seduce the unstable; they are experts in greed – an accursed brood! (verse 14). This verse makes the point even more strongly and stresses their continual sinning and the sexual nature of their sin. The form this sexual sin took is not described, though the next verse uses Balaam as an example and that might point towards the nature of the sexual sin involved. At the heart of their teaching is a greedy appetite, no doubt for money, but also for all the so-called 'pleasures' of life. (Balaam was noted both for his seduction of the Israelites to sexual immorality with the Moabites and also for his financial greed.)

The seductive nature of their activities and their teaching is particularly dangerous for the church. The whole picture Peter paints is of what we might call a hedonistic life-style.[30]

> **They have left the straight way and wandered off to follow the way of Balaam son of Beor, who loved the wages of wickedness. But he was rebuked for his wrongdoing by a donkey – a beast without speech – who spoke with a man's voice and restrained the prophet's madness** (verses 15-16).

Balaam, an example also used by Jude, seems at first to be a strange choice as he received genuine communications from God and, at least to begin with, stood against accepting bribes (Numbers 22:1-20). Balak, king of the Moabites, wanted Balaam to curse the Israelites who were beginning to take over the land. Balaam refused to do so. Eventually, Balaam did decide to go to Balak but his donkey refused to go in that direction because he saw an angel of the Lord standing in the path (Numbers 22:21-25). Eventually the Lord allowed Balaam also to see the angel of the Lord who told him only to prophesy what the Lord God told him. Rather than putting a curse on the Israelites, he blessed them (Numbers 23–24). Balak did not like this at all, and eventually Balaam returned home.

---

30. The word translated 'pleasure' in the second part of verse 13 comes from the same Greek root *hedone* as our words 'hedonist' or 'hedonism'.

Even a donkey understood more of God's will in these matters than Balaam did; so Peter's comparison is that, like Balaam, these false teachers have no understanding of the Lord and his will. Indeed they are worse than the **brute beasts** and **creatures of instinct** which he had called them back in verse 12!

In Numbers 25 the narrative moves immediately to describing how the Israelites were seduced to worship other gods and to become involved in sexual promiscuity with the Moabites. Although Numbers 23–24 tells us nothing of Balaam's part in this seduction of Israel, we read in Numbers 31 that Balaam had urged this course of action on the Moabites (31:8, 16). Thousands of Israelites were judged for their sin, immorality and pagan worship. In Revelation 2:14 Jesus, writing to the church at Pergamum, refers to people who hold the same teaching as Balaam who enticed 'the Israelites to sin by eating food sacrificed to idols and by committing sexual immorality'. This, no doubt, is also in Peter's mind in these verses. Just as Balaam had a role in the seduction of the Israelites into sexual sin with Moabite women, so these false teachers and leaders were seeking to seduce Christians with a sexually promiscuous and hedonistic life-style. Balaam certainly provides a good lesson from Scripture of the depth of sin into which the false teachers had fallen.

b) They are empty and useless (verses 17-22)

These men are springs without water and mists driven by a storm. Blackest darkness is reserved for them. For they mouth empty boastful words and, by appealing to the lustful desires of sinful human nature, they entice people who are just escaping from those who live in error (verses 17-18).

As Peter continues with his warnings against these evil men, he once again stresses the judgment that awaits such heretics

– **blackest darkness is reserved for them**. He also demonstrates the essential bankruptcy of their positions. They are **springs without water**. We have a house in Wales which gets its water from a natural spring. When we bought the house, no matter what the brochure said about how good this water tasted, the first real test came in a long hot summer. The spring continued to provide us with water, though at a reduced level. A spring without water is worthless and ultimately has no purpose. This is the vacuous nature of these people Peter confronts. In the same way, in that long hot summer a few years ago, as the spring was producing less and less water each day, the early morning mists provided no help at all. **... mists driven by a storm**. We needed storms to produce rain, not simply to blow mist around. The pictures Peter uses are vivid and understandable to us all.

Teachers need to provide what is useful and edifying for a Christian congregation. These men mouth **empty and boastful words** of no use to anyone. Nevertheless they do know how to attract people to their ways. They simply play to the sinful nature – **appealing to the lustful desires of sinful human nature**. All are open to temptation and this fact was being exploited.

Never must Christians forget the deep theological truth Peter is drawing upon here. So many Christians think they are above such temptations to sin. With salvation secured by God's grace and favour to them, it is easy to begin to believe that temptation can readily be resisted.

Two elements combined to make this early church particularly susceptible to such temptations to sexual sin. First, many of the congregation were **just escaping from those who live in error**. In other words, many were new converts from paganism. They had been used to such feasts and orgies and self-indulgence in their former non-Christian lives. No doubt they missed what they had left behind. To be told that

such things were permissible left them specially open to seduction
away from the truth of Scripture. Secondly, the congregation
was facing a direct appeal to particular temptations to **lustful
desires** that affect almost everyone. To be told that one of
the most common and basic desires of the sinful human nature
is actually admissible would be temptation indeed!

Special Lessons for Today

This portrayal of the church to which Peter writes gives us
much food for thought. As we think of some of the greatest
temptations and problems faced by church congregations
today, surely we would include much of what he has
highlighted. For example, we see hedonism all around us.
Many in our churches are also new converts from a pagan
society in which sexual sin and even sexual perversion are
not regarded as morally wrong and where hedonism generally
is the philosophy of the day (at least in practice). A church
living in a culture like ours and with many new first generation
converts is particularly susceptible to false teachers like those
Peter faced. Human nature is sinful and has not changed since
Peter's day!

It is important not to overlook just how easily we can be
tempted, if not actually into particular sins, at least to the
point where we no longer regard such behaviour as
particularly sinful for others. The other day I talked to a
Christian teenager who had been to a Christian friend's
eighteenth birthday party. Large amounts of alcohol were
brought along, some by Christian teenagers. Two youngsters
had to be helped back home because they were so drunk.
What was most worrying about the incident was not so much
the drinking and drunkenness, which could at least partly be
blamed on the fact that some non-Christians had 'laced' the
drinks, but the fact that several Christian teenagers could not
see the problem with what had happened. Older Christians

had not set a good example, for they had not indicated clearly what they regarded as wrong or ungodly behaviour. Boundaries are being deliberately blurred. Is it any wonder the younger generation of teenagers can seem confused about holiness?

Sexual sin also pervades some church congregations and often receives the blessing of false leaders in various denominations. The practice of homosexual sexual acts is condemned in Scripture, but society would not agree and it takes courage to stand against the tide, specially when people are being converted to Christ from such a life-style and may have particular temptations in that direction. But while that sin may sometimes be highlighted, it is easy to forget that Christian leaders often seem happy to excuse serial adultery, otherwise known as multiple divorces. Co-habitation without marriage is acceptable and even justified by many leaders on the grounds that this is how society now is! And so we could go on. But here as so often with sinful human nature, we can all too easily point the finger at others while ignoring the way in which we too are seduced into sexual sin or other forms of hedonistic pleasure seeking.

We live in an age which teaches us that the most important thing in life is to look after 'self'. How quickly this becomes little more than self indulgence, and we have seen clearly what little time Peter has for this sort of behaviour. This passage reminds us that Peter expects a holy life-style of Christian people. Self is not at the centre. Christ is to be at the centre, and if he is, we shall find ourselves beginning to look beyond ourselves to love and to serve him more deeply and to love our neighbour as ourselves. Perhaps as churches we need to worry less about 'self-esteem' and more about 'Christ esteem' and we would once again not be so easily seduced by the jargon and ideas of the world. How we live for God and who is at the centre of our lives is as significant as what we might teach about the centrality of Christ.

Finally, let us also remember just how important in a church's life is good teaching. More and more churches are following the ways of the world and regarding teaching with indifference. It is alright for those who want it, but it is not an essential part of Christian life. Far more important is how we *feel* about our faith and about the Lord Jesus. Our feelings about Jesus and our faith are of course very important. But our feelings can sin as much as our minds can sin or our bodies can sin. Teaching is vital if we are to recognise what sin is and what our temptations are. We need to be looking for and affirming church leaders who give a high priority in their ministries to teaching the word of God. In our own lives we need to seek them out as the people most likely to resist the seduction of the world as they teach and, with God's help, live by the Word.

They promise them freedom, while they themselves are slaves of depravity – for a man is a slave of whatever has mastered him (verse 19).

In 1:4 Peter had talked of how Christians can **escape the corruption of the world caused by evil desires**. This was the true freedom which Peter has in mind here. To be free from the corruption that our sinful human nature always seeks to draw us towards is freedom indeed. Hand in hand with this, for the Christian, goes a freedom from final judgment. But while they promise such freedom, these leaders are, in fact, mastered by their sinful nature, their **depravity**.[31] In other words they remain slaves to another master.[32] In Matthew 6:24 Jesus put it like this: 'No one can serve two masters.

---

31. The word is otherwise translated as 'corruption' in 1:4 and refers to perishing in the final destruction of the world in 2:12.

32. See Romans 6:12-14 where the apostle Paul also compares the mastery of sin with the mastery of God in the Christian's life.

Either he will hate the one and love the other, or he will be devoted to the one and despise the other.' Only as we serve the Lord do we find true freedom. The Book of Common Prayer of the Church of England sums it up so clearly in the phrase– 'in whose service is perfect freedom'. Such freedom in service is part and parcel of being a holy people, a point Peter had already made back in 1 Peter 2:15-16.

These false teachers claimed to have freedom but in fact, in not obeying Christ, found themselves serving their own selfish ends of depravity. They were so mastered by their depravity that they were even creating a theology to justify their behaviour. Their lives reveal the lie they are promoting, again helping true believers recognise false teachers.

It is a much neglected but vital point of doctrine that Peter draws upon here. Just as he has insisted that human nature is sinful, so now he insists that *there is no neutrality before God*. Our teaching and our behaviour in life together will indicate whether we are mastered by Christ, and hence truly enjoying 'freedom', or whether we are mastered by depravity and sin. Neutrality often goes hand in hand with tolerance as the most acceptable approach to the great moral issues of life. Neutrality is simply not a Christian option as we face the seduction of hedonistic pleasures.

If they have escaped the corruption of the world by knowing our Lord and Saviour Jesus Christ and are again entangled in it and overcome, they are worse off at the end than they were at the beginning. It would have been better for them not to have known the way of righteousness, than to have known it and then to turn their backs on the sacred command that was passed on to them. Of them the proverbs are true: 'A dog returns to its vomit,' and, 'A sow that is washed goes back to her wallowing in the mud' (verses 20-22).

These last three verses talk of those who know Jesus but return to their former way of life. The first question to be addressed is whether Peter is referring to those new Christians (end of verse 18) who are being pulled back to their former ways of error, or to the false teachers themselves who have known Jesus but are now living as those entangled once again in a sinful life. While there is much to be said for either view, the flow of Peter's argument throughout the chapter is that the false teachers will be judged. The immediately preceding verses have been describing the false teachers and verse 20 begins in the Greek with the little word 'for' which links it directly with verse 19 which has been describing the false teachers. For these reasons, it seems likely that verses 20-22 should be taken as referring to the heretical leaders.

These people are in particularly serious danger because they **have escaped the corruption of the world by knowing our Lord and Saviour Jesus Christ**. Indeed they **are worse off** now than if they had never known. This statement raises a number of questions for us. Were these people ever really committed to Christ as Lord? Is it assumed that they will now be judged by God? If so, how do we understand this Scripture in the light of other passages that indicate that once people belong to Christ they always belong to him, for he both knows them and *keeps* them (e.g. John 10:27-29; Romans 8:30)? Indeed, the questions raised are not unlike those examined when looking at 2:1 earlier.

Some commentators and Christian teachers believe there are several passages in Scripture which indicate that true Christians can indeed apostasize and finally be condemned by God rather than be saved. They point to passages like Hebrews 6:4-6 or to John 15:1-7 where it appears that genuine branches are 'cut off' the vine if they bear no fruit. The debate over whether or not it is possible for one who has definitely been a 'saved' Christian to fall away into final damnation will no doubt continue. Christians who believe Scripture to be reliable and true take different views on this matter.

The fact that there are passages that seem to present different perspectives on this matter should encourage us first and foremost to be humble in presenting our interpretation. The Bible is infallible as God's word, but I as an interpreter am not and need to be prepared to change my views if I can be shown from Scripture that my views are wrong. Second, we should be very careful to look at a text both in its immediate context (the verse, paragraph, book), and its larger context (the Petrine corpus, the New Testament, the Bible as a whole). Third, we may well want to see if there are other Scriptures that can actually begin to help us harmonise what may appear to be teachings at odds with each other.

In this context, it has to be said that Peter uses a similar vocabulary to that which speaks of becoming a Christian back in 1:3-4. For example, the words 'through knowledge of him' (1:3) closely resemble 'by knowing our Lord' in 2:20. Also the words 'escape the corruption' (1:4) closely resemble the words 'escaped the corruption' in 2:20.[33] However, as we read on we find that Peter is going to put these false teachers firmly in the context of the 'signs of the times'. He will argue that it is a sign of the 'last days' that such people are at work in the world (3:3), and that the apostles and the Lord himself had warned of this.

As we look to the Gospels and Jesus' own teaching, we find some pointers that may help us understand what Peter is saying. In Matthew 7:15-20 Jesus points out that trees that do not bear good fruit will be cut down and thrown into the fire. It becomes immediately clear, however, that such 'trees' are not actually *real* trees! Jesus continues: 'Not everyone who says to me, "Lord, Lord," will enter the kingdom of heaven.... Many will say to me on that day, "Lord, Lord, did we not prophesy in your name, and in your name drive out

---

33. The words translated 'corruption' in the New International Version are not the same in the Greek, though both are correctly translated 'corruption'.

demons and perform many miracles?" Then I will tell them
plainly, "I never knew you. Away from me you evildoers!" '
(7:21-23).

Jesus' description well fits the type of false prophets and
teachers that Peter was facing. Such people will *appear* to be
full Christians. They will know in their head, at least, the
whole truth of salvation. For a while they even may have
genuinely moved to a different moral stance in which they
could be said to 'have escaped the corruption of the world'.
Indeed, by mixing among Christians they would have done
that, surely. But now their true colours are emerging. They
are to be known by their fruit. The reality of their apparent
commitment to following Christ will be seen in the way they
live and the teachings they propound, not simply by their
claim to be Christians.

Peter says these people, then, have become **entangled**
again in the corruption and have been **overcome**. The picture
reminds us of those Jesus describes in the parable of the sower
who were swamped by the thorns of this world ('worries of
this life, the deceitfulness of wealth and the desires for other
things', Mark 4:19). Such people are worse off than those
who had never **known the way of righteousness**. And again
we see Peter surely drawing upon the teachings of Jesus to
which he will refer in 3:2. He uses almost the same words as
Jesus used in Matthew 12:45 when he was talking of a demon
being cast out of a person. When nothing replaces it, it returns
with seven other spirits and 'the final condition of that man
is worse than the first'. Judgment will surely be worse for
those who hear and know the truth and then deliberately **turn
their backs on the sacred command that was passed on to
them**, than it will be for the pagan who has never known.
This **command** refers to the whole gospel of salvation in
Jesus Christ that has been passed to them.

The sayings, no doubt well known to Peter's audience,

are clear enough. A dog vomits and returns to its vomit. A pig may appear to wash itself in clean water only to return very soon to the mud from which it came. Neither animal would have been highly regarded in those days, and again it reminds us of Peter's earlier statement that these false leaders are like **brute beasts** (v 12). Undoubtedly they are empty and useless.

It is perhaps one of the saddest experiences Christians can have when they see someone they thought was a genuine believer showing once and for all by their behaviour or by their teaching that they were never really genuine in their commitment to Christ and faith in him. Why some people behave like this we shall never know. Perhaps for some, like these false leaders, there was a pride and arrogance in leading people in a new religion and being looked up to by others. Perhaps others we meet in life find some initial comfort in the gospel message. It sounds attractive, and can appear to offer a comfortable route to deal with the pressures of the world, but whenever real commitment is mentioned, whenever they are asked to take a stand, whenever the demand for holiness contradicts the pull of self-indulgence, then some simply give up on the faith. More dangerous are those who, as in Peter's day, do not give up on the faith but adapt the faith, the **sacred command**, to suit their pleasure and then seduce others to follow them. We would be naive if we did not recognise that this can happen today all too easily.

This chapter began by warning the readers of the danger of false prophets who teach heresies and yet are very capable of attracting others with their ideas. Their condemnation is certainly sealed. However, Christians need to remember the truth of Peter's gospel and ensure that they know how to recognise false teachers when they appear. These teachers are hedonistic blasphemers and are useless spiritually.

The Flood in Noah's day and the destruction of Sodom

and Gomorrah are used by Peter to emphasise the seriousness
of the subject with which he is dealing. But these examples
serve two further purposes. They point to the judgment and
condemnation that awaits such evil people. They also remind
true believers, who are finding it difficult to remain constant
in the faith, that God rescued the righteous and so will stand
by them and rescue them from such evil, in fulfilment of his
precious promises to them.

Excursus: Michael, an accusation and the dispute over the body of Moses.

If, in 2:11, Peter has at the back of his mind what is explicit
in Jude 9, then it may be helpful to try to piece together the
account of the archangel Michael and Moses and the devil.
The death and burial of Moses are mentioned in the Old
Testament, but there is no mention of any dispute between
Michael and the Devil about the matter. In Deuteronomy 34:6
we are told that God buried the body of Moses in Moab near
Beth Peor and that no one knows where the body was buried.

Michael (Jude 9), whose name means 'Who is like God?',
is mentioned in the Books of Daniel and of Revelation. In
Daniel 10:13, 21 there is a reference to 'Michael, one of the
chief princes' who was involved in helping the people of
Israel during the time of the Babylonian captivity. Later in
chapter 12:1 Michael is mentioned as the one who will arise
in the last days. He is 'the great prince who protects [the]
people [of God]'. The reference in 1 Thessalonians 4:16 to
an 'archangel' who will appear with Christ at the end of time
is almost certainly another reference to Michael. In Revelation
12:7, we are told that 'Michael and his angels fought against
the dragon' and won, so that the dragon (Satan) lost his place
in heaven together with his own angels who followed him.

'The Lord rebuke you!' (Jude 9) is a reference to Zechariah
3:2 where it is set in the context of a vision of a courtroom

scene. There a high priest called Joshua stands before 'an angel of the LORD' (verse 1), and Satan stands beside Joshua to accuse him. In the courtroom drama there is a fascinating example of one who, though a high priest, is a sinner. Satan fulfils his role of accusing God's people of sin, but the angel steps forward to say that Joshua's sin has been removed, and so we read, 'The LORD rebuke you, Satan!'

This is the extent of the Biblical information. Our problem, therefore, in understanding all this is that nowhere in the Bible, except in Jude, do these references appear to come together nor are they made to fit in with each other. However, in a number of intertestamental Jewish writings, Satan is regarded as the accuser who tries to undo or challenge the work of God's people and of 'the angel of the Lord'. The problem of understanding these two verses in Jude was nearly as acute for the very early New Testament commentators as it is for us. But they had before them another piece of Jewish writing known as the *Testament of Moses*. We only have a late Latin version of this document, but Clement of Alexandria, Origen and other early Christian writers seem to have had a complete and longer writing, probably in Hebrew or Aramaic, from which they believed Jude drew the story he used here.

Richard Bauckham in his commentary[34] on this epistle has sought carefully to reconstruct from various sources what the 'lost ending' of this document may have said about Moses and Satan and the dispute over the body. The original story was clearly based on Scripture but included other details. Moses died before entering the Promised Land. God used the archangel Michael to bury Moses in some unknown place. Satan, however, with his usual malice and antagonism towards God's people, accused Moses of being a dreadful sinner for murdering an Egyptian and therefore sought to deny Moses a proper burial. This slanderous accusation was made before

33. Bauckham, R., *Jude, 2 Peter*, Word Biblical Commentary, Vol 50, 1983.

Michael who, instead of rebuking Satan himself, responded by saying to Satan: 'The Lord rebuke you!' When Satan finally left, Michael took the body and buried it in a place that no one knows. In other words, Jude's point is to establish that, even in the most serious of circumstances where accusation would seem justified, this was left entirely to God himself. Not even Michael took this upon himself.

Peter may be building on all this background. However, he does not develop the ideas as Jude does, and he certainly does not make a big issue of his point. Much more important to him is the fact that the false teachers are speaking against angels and saying things about them of which they have no understanding. They are 'bold and arrogant' when they should rather be afraid of those who take their orders directly from God.[35]

6. Remember – Christ will return (3:1-16)

Dear friends, this is now my second letter to you. I have written both of them as reminders to stimulate you to wholesome thinking (verse 1).

Chapter 3 begins with a recapitulation of the teaching that Peter most wants his audience to take to heart. It partly summarises his concerns with false teachers, but it also firmly sets the church in the context of the last days.[36] In doing this Peter brings encouragement as well as warning. This encouragement lies in remembering what the prophets and the Lord himself spoke about the time in which they were

---

35. Note: this excursus also appears later in the commentary on Jude in order to allow the commentaries to be read and studied separately.

36. This context, though not developed, was firmly established in 1:11. The many links between chapters 1-2 and chapter 3 suggest a continuous letter (contra commentators who believe that chapters 1-2 may be the 'first' letter Peter alludes to, and chapter 3 the 'second letter', 3:1.)

now living. It also lies in recalling the nature of God himself, his creative word, his eternity, his sovereign rule even over evil, his patience, his faithfulness in keeping his promises, and his desire that all should come to repentance. Encouragement for the Christian is also to be found in remembering that the day that brings judgment for the unbeliever and the false teacher brings, for the believer, a new heaven and a new earth, the home of righteousness. All of this should provide still further encouragement not to follow the false teachers but to seek to live a life of holiness rooted in growth in grace and the knowledge of the Lord and Saviour Jesus Christ.

Being reminded of faith and life in this context is a sure stimulation to **wholesome thinking**. Since 2:3 Peter has not directly addressed his audience. Rather he has described in detail the false teachings of the heretics and referred to 'these men' and 'they'. Of course the description has all been part of his warning to the faithful Christians in the church, but as he moves back to address them in a more personal way as he did in the first chapter, he speaks again of 'you' and of 'us' and 'we'.

Dear friends marks this change to a warm-hearted and passionate appeal to the faithful in the church. It also reminds us of the warmth of his approach to these people in his first letter (1 Peter 2:11; 4:12). This form of address is used again in verses 8, 14 and 17 and might better be translated as 'well loved people' or 'well loved friends'.

However, as we noted in the Introduction, **my second letter to you** need not refer back to what we now have as 1 Peter. There may have been another letter between 1 and 2 Peter. Or, indeed, it is possible that the destinations of what we know as 1 Peter and 2 Peter were different. In either case Peter would then be referring to a letter which has not come down to us.

a) Remember the words of the prophets and of Christ (verses 1-2)

I want you to recall the words spoken in the past by the holy prophets and the command given by our Lord and Saviour through your[37] apostles (verse 2).

In the opening two verses of this chapter, Peter indicates to the reader that he is once again picking up themes he had mentioned in the first chapter. He stresses the need to 'recall' (verse 2; compare 1:12-13) and to 'understand' (verse 3; compare 1:20).

Understanding what the Bible says, that is, what the **holy prophets** have spoken, and what **our Lord and Saviour** himself has said, will be the only full-proof way of combating heresy. This was a theme in the first epistle (e.g. 1 Peter 1:10-12; 2:4-12 etc.), and is a vital message for all churches through the ages. It is assumed that it is **through [the] apostles** that we can know exactly and reliably what Jesus had spoken and commanded.

Of course, the particular **words spoken in the past** that Peter wishes them to remember are those relating to the final day of salvation, the 'day of the Lord'. Peter himself clearly lives by the principle he is enunciating. He looks to Scripture and to apostolic teaching, including his own, as finally authoritative in all matters. We need only remember back to his speech on the day of Pentecost to see how he proves his teaching about Jesus by looking back over Old Testament teaching. Or again we can look at his significant use of the words of the prophets in 1 Peter 2:4-8.

Peter's mention of the **command** given by Christ reminds

---

37. Some have suggested that your apostles implies that the writer himself could not have been an apostle. This, it is said, adds weight to the view that the letter was not written by Peter but by someone who followed the apostolic generation. However, there is no need to assume this. The sentence can be read simply to refer to those apostles who first brought the message of Jesus to these particular Christians to whom Peter is now writing.

us of 2:21. As we saw there it refers to the whole gospel of
Jesus as passed on to the New Testament churches by the
apostles. But here Peter is specially interested in the teaching
of Jesus relating to ethics and behaviour in the context of the
last days. The heretics 'scoff' (verse 3) at such teachings.

b) Many scoff at such teaching (verses 3-4)

**First of all you must understand that in the last days scoffers
will come, scoffing and following their own evil desires** (verse 3).

The last days are those days between the first coming of
Christ and the second. On the day of Pentecost Peter himself
had used the prophecy from Joel to indicate that the last days
had now come: 'In the last days, God says, I will pour out my
Spirit on all people' (Acts 2:17; see Joel 2:28-32). From that
time onwards until the day of the Lord, the church would be
living in the last days.

First of all you must understand ... As these Christians
confront a world and even church leaders who are scoffing at
the notion of a holy life and even at the idea that Christ will
return, Peter wants God's people to understand **first** from
Scripture that all this was prophesied. The prophets had
warned of scoffers, and the apostles and even Jesus himself
had warned believers that false teachers and **scoffers will
come**.[38] Those prophecies were now coming true in the church
to which Peter was writing, but, more than that, scoffing at
such teaching was to become a hallmark for Christians of
life in the last days.

... following their own evil desires raises again the issue
Peter has addressed throughout the letter. It is perhaps
inevitable that those who should mock the Word of God and

---

38. For example, see Psalm 73:7-11; Isaiah 5:18-19; Jeremiah 17:15;
Habakkuk 1:5 quoted in Acts 13:41; 1 Peter 4:13-15; also Jesus' warnings
against false teachers e.g., Matthew 5:11; Mark 13:21-23.

deny the return of Christ, as we shall see in verse 3, will also take no notice of the command for holiness, choosing rather to follow their evil desires. The Greek word translated here as 'evil desires' is the word Peter uses to summarise the behaviour of the false teachers (1:4; 2:10, 18).

> **They will say, "Where is this 'coming' he promised? Ever since our[39] fathers died, everything goes on as it has since the beginning of creation"** (verse 4).

Christ has not yet returned. We now live 2000 years on from Christ's first coming and still he has not come. Perhaps it should not surprise us that the teaching of Christ's return is mocked in our day and age. But such mockery started very early. Thirty or so years was still a long time. A generation had passed away in that time. Those who had been household leaders and political leaders in Jesus' day, the middle-aged and older, had already died and still he had not come. Indeed, it is quite possible that 'the fathers' of this church, the apostles

---

39. The Greek does not include the word 'our' but has 'the fathers'. This reference to 'the fathers' is seen by Richard Bauckham (*Jude, 2 Peter*, p. 290-291) and other recent commentators as evidence that the apostolic generation (the fathers) had by this time died and therefore the author of 2 Peter could not be the apostle Peter. At least two possible responses to this suggest themselves. First, whereas 'the fathers' is a common way of referring to the Old Testament leaders and prophets, it is not (as far as I can discover) used elsewhere in first century or even early second century literature of the apostolic generation. Translations which insert the word 'our', as in the New International Version, may therefore be giving the right feel to Peter's intention. Many senior church leaders and teachers from those early post Pentecost days would undoubtedly have died in the intervening 30 years, even if the younger apostles had not yet died. Indeed a number of the apostles may well have died as well and perhaps even the apostles responsible for planting this very church. The fact of the matter is that the Bible is silent on when most of the apostles died. Assuming that Peter wrote this epistle, we may also assume that Paul was still alive and certainly that John was still alive, but not much more can be said reliably about the death or otherwise of others from that generation.

and early leaders who had 'planted' the church had now died, and so the younger heretical leaders ask: 'So where is this "coming" '?

We must not underestimate the power of this challenge to the Christian faith. It is all too easy for a question like this to raise doubts in the mind of even the most sincere believer. When asked with passion by teachers like those being confronted in this epistle, the criticism of traditional teaching can seem very strong indeed. There is only one way to provide an answer to and protection from such scoffing and that is to trust the promises of God in Scripture and to understand that such scoffing will be inevitable as people reject those promises.

c) Be assured – he will come to judge (verses 5-7)

> **But they deliberately forget that long ago by God's word the heavens existed and the earth was formed out of water and by water. By these waters also the world of that time was deluged and destroyed. By the same word the present heavens and earth are reserved for fire, being kept for the day of judgment and destruction of ungodly men** (verses 5-6).

This is Peter's last significant comment about the position of the heretics. In a moment he will turn to draw encouragement

---

Secondly, the fact that 'the fathers' was a common way to refer to the people of the Old Testament (see for example John 6:31 and 1 Corinthians 10:1), it is at least possible that this was what the heretics had in mind. The fathers (in the Old Testament) had prophesied the 'day of the Lord', the 'coming' that would bring judgment. Indeed it seems that there had been such talk since the very start of the world but it had never happened, so they mock. This second view, that 'the fathers' looks back to the prophets and leaders of the Old Testament, is given some support from the second part of verse 4 in which the scoffers take us right back to creation and argue that everything is going on just as it always has. (This second view is adopted by Simon Kistemaker in his commentary, p. 326.)

for believers from the doctrine of Christ's return. At the heart of heretical teaching of any sort is the denial of God's spoken and active word. Peter contrasts the way true believers should 'remember' God's word (verse 2) and the fact that the heretics **forget** that word. However, simply to 'forget' the word might imply a degree of failure but not of false teaching and heretical belief. Peter argues that these scoffing teachers know the word and have **deliberately** forgotten bits that they don't like or think are irrelevant. How often we find Christians today who overlook the bits of Scripture that do not suit what they want to believe or do not fit with their actions. This was the problem faced by Peter and the believers in this church.

1) God's word creates

... by God's word. Peter points out now that the very word of God that they choose deliberately to forget is God's *active* word. God's word cannot be treated as purely theoretical. It is not simply to be reduced to a set of doctrines that can be accepted or deliberately ignored. It was by his word that **the heavens existed and the earth was formed out of water and by water**. God's word doesn't just provide us with a doctrine of creation that can be side-stepped, but it actually *creates*. 'And God said, "Let there be light," and there was light' (Genesis 1:3). It is a word that has brought into being and a word that always fulfils promises as well as actually making those promises. To say that we believe and trust God's word must also directly involve a commitment to the power of that word to bring to pass whatever is promised.[40]

The words **formed out of water and by water** look back to the first chapter of Genesis as well, specially verses 6 and 9-10. We read that in dividing the waters God created the earth. This is not a scientific explanation of how it all took place, but simply reminds us that water had a part to play in

---

40. Hebrews 11:3 says: 'the universe was formed at God's command.'

the way God brought the earth into being. And that leads very naturally into Peter's next point.

2) God's word destroys
This word that has created is also a word that has destroyed. It is vital that we see the importance of what Peter is saying here: deliberately forgetting the *creating* word of God is part and parcel of their attempt to hide the *destroying* (judging) word of God.

By these waters also the world of that time was deluged and destroyed. Just as water had been used in creation at the order of God so it was used in the destruction of the earth in Noah's day (see 2:5). God's word is so active and powerful that he spoke and the world was destroyed through the great flood (Genesis 6:7; 7:4, 23).

In verse 7 Peter drives home for the believers the quite devastating message that the heretics who deny Christ's coming will be judged when he comes. **By the same word**, that is by the active word of God, **the present heavens and earth are reserved for fire, being kept for the day of judgment and destruction of ungodly men**.

Just as in the past God's word had been seen to create the world and then bring about the destruction of ungodly people (2:5), so now God's word stands that he will destroy the heavens and earth by fire. God will judge. God has spoken. It has not yet happened, but Peter wants his readers to know that God's word is as sure now as it has been in the past. God always brings about his spoken will and he does so **by the same word**.

reserved for fire ... But has God spoken of destruction by fire up to this point in history? Remember that back in verse 2 Peter was drawing attention to words spoken in the past in the prophets and by Jesus himself that have come down to us through the apostles. As we look back through the prophets we find many references to judgment by fire. In some instances it seems limited to a refining type of judgment for the people of God, but in other places it is far more general and even universal in its application. For example in Isaiah 66, a passage that looks forward to the coming of the Lord, we read this:

> 'See, the LORD is coming with fire, and his chariots are like a whirlwind; he will bring down his anger with fury, and his rebuke with flames of fire. For with fire and with his sword the LORD will execute judgment upon all men.... "And I [declares the LORD], because of their actions and their imaginations, am about to come and gather all nations and tongues, and they will come and see my glory.... As the new heavens and the new earth that I make will endure before me," declares the LORD, "so will your name and descendents endure.... And they will go out and look upon the dead bodies of those who rebelled against me; their worm will not die, nor will their fire be quenched..." ' (from Isaiah 66:15-24).

Given Peter's reference to 'a new heaven and a new earth' (3:13), it seems to me to be entirely likely that he had this chapter in Isaiah in mind as the main word of the Lord concerning the future judgment that the false leaders were deliberately ignoring. But we may also note Malachi 4:1 and Zephaniah 1:18 and a number of other passages which also talk of destruction by fire.

However, the words of Jesus and of the apostles should also have been well known by any Christian teacher. For example, Jesus explains the parable of the weeds in Matthew 13:39-42 as a reference to the end of the age when he says, 'the weeds are pulled up and burned in the fire, so it will be at the end of the age'. Even the apostles had spoken on the subject. For example, the apostle Paul refers to the fire of the last day in 1 Corinthians 3:13 (though here it is a refining fire sorting out the works of believers). While we do not know whether Hebrews had been written by the time Peter wrote his epistle, it is specially interesting to note that the author has to tackle a very similar situation in which people deliberately sin even after they 'have received a knowledge of the truth'. His approach to what will happen to these people is much the same as Peter's: 'no sacrifice for sin is left, but only a fearful expectation of judgment and of raging fire that will consume the enemies of God' (Hebrews 10:26-27).

While true believers are being rescued by the Lord, these unbelievers are **being kept for the day of judgment**. This is the day of Christ's return which will see the **destruction of ungodly men** (look at 2:9). There is no doubt these false teachers Peter addressed had the word of God on the matter of sin such as theirs and their eventual end. But they scoffed at such ideas.

Special Lessons for Today
The applications of these verses to today's world and even today's church are numerous and sadly all too obvious. Heretics have not learned their lesson. Scorn is still poured on those who believe in God's word and therefore believe that a judgment day will come as certainly as Noah's flood happened, as certainly as God's active word always carries through on his promises.

The importance of the Second Coming as a matter of faith remains as vital today as ever. The Second Coming holds out to believers the promise of eternity with Christ, a day we look forward to (verse 12). But it also reminds us that the old earth and old heaven will be destroyed and that fire will be used in judgment of those who have deliberately rejected the word of God. Belief in the Second Coming is not popular even among many Christians today. Perhaps we have subconsciously swallowed some of the false teaching that abounds, a teaching that suggests the whole language involved is mythological and simply pointing to God's general working for good in his world. But the language of Scripture as a whole, the prophets, Jesus and the apostles, stresses again and again the reality of the 'day of the Lord' as an extraordinary event that will occur at a time in history.

We are to live in the light of that amazing truth. For the believer it becomes an incentive, (i) to live a holy life and be ready (see verses 11-14), and (ii) to engage in evangelism. If I believe that unforgiven sinners will suffer judgment of this sort, surely I will be the more motivated to take the Good News of the forgiveness and love of Christ to them. For the unbeliever or heretical syncretistic teacher that day is certainly coming and the prospect should cause them to turn in repentance to the living Lord whose return is guaranteed by God's unfailing promises in Scripture.

These short verses (1-7) also remind us of the great dangers for all Christians of ignoring those Scriptures which we do not like. Scripture is reduced to those passages which we *can* believe, or which we *want* to obey. Where they contradict the beliefs of this world that we have absorbed, then we ignore them. Indeed, because we know the Bible, we find ourselves deliberately ignoring God's word. We have all been warned, and this is certainly a temptation for everyone, which is why those false teachers Peter addressed seemed to have been somewhat successful in seducing people away from the Word.

Thirdly, we cannot pass over the fact that Peter assumes a judgment on the basis that God's word spoke in the past and delivered in the past and therefore will deliver in the future. The example he uses is of Noah's flood. In many Christian circles these days, it has become almost fashionable to talk of that part of Genesis which describes the flood as 'mythological'. While that word has many meanings to different people, we need to be careful what we do with the flood. Peter believed God created and God destroyed, therefore we know he can create a new heaven and a new

earth. And we know he will destroy again because he has
promised to do so. Whether or not one takes a 'seven day
creationist' perspective or believes in a 'universal flood' in
Noah's day, it is important to note that where people
'demythologise' these events and suggest they never actually
happened in history (but perhaps are simply stories told to
reveal theological truth of some sort), there we often find the
greatest scepticism concerning the return of Christ. Among
such people we often find the greatest tendency to dismiss
the possibility of a consuming eternal fire of hell. Indeed,
many I have talked to who demythologise Genesis 1-11 also
scorn any literal understanding of judgment at the return of
Christ.

This is not to suggest that Genesis gives us a scientific
statement about *how* creation took place or *how* the flood
happened. I am not denying that metaphorical language can
be used in Scripture in many places to describe the Second
Coming of Christ, but we need to make our decisions about
these matters on the basis of our study of God's Word
(Scripture) rather than because it fits better with modern
scientific theory, or because it fits better with our view of a
loving God, or whatever. If we treat the Bible as the infallible
word of God, and if we believe in a God whose word is always
active and delivers on his promises, then we should interpret
Scripture with great care, and be prepared to alter our beliefs
and our lives accordingly when they are challenged by what
we read. Peter's understanding of Scripture is that God's word
concerning the return of Christ to judge and to usher in a new
heaven and a new earth is as sure as his word was when he
sent the Flood in Noah's day and destroyed all creation, save
that which he had placed in the ark. This should also be our
understanding.

d) The timing of Christ's return (verses 8-10)

As Peter continues to speak to the believers, his **dear friends**, he asks them to remember (see verses 1-2) another important point that will help them address the problem raised by the heretics. The delay in the return of the Lord does not mean that it will not happen.

> **But do not forget this one thing, dear friends: With the Lord a day is like a thousand years, and a thousand years are like a day. The Lord is not slow in keeping his promise, as some understand slowness. He is patient with you, not wanting any to perish, but everyone to come to repentance** (verses 8-9).

Peter has argued that God's word guarantees the return but, even so, the delay was as perplexing for believers then as it is today. And so Peter tackles the issue head on, asking us to bear in mind two points.

i) *God's timing*. This point is simple. We should not simply look at time from our point of view. We need to remember just who this eternal God is before we jump to conclusions about describing the delay as a 'long time'.

ii) *God's purposes*. We need to remember that God's purposes for the future do not simply concern judgment and salvation on the last day, but also concern people's salvation being worked out right now. If that all takes time, then we can put it down to God's patience with sinful people as he desires their repentance.

With the Lord a day is like a thousand years, and a thousand years are like a day recalls the words of Psalm 90:4 – 'For a thousand years in your sight are like a day that has just gone by, or like a watch in the night'. Of course Peter is not arguing, as some have suggested, that wherever we read 'day' in the Bible we can substitute 'a thousand years'. We cannot, for example, suggest that the six days of creation are in fact to be understood as 6000 years! Peter's point is actually much simpler than that. He is asking his readers to recognise that God is God and we are human beings for whom seventy years is a life-time!

We need to remember that God may take what seems to us to be an inordinately long time to fulfil his promises, but then he is God! Certainly the fact that he is eternal in his existence should reinforce this point for us. However, we need to be careful that Peter is not saying that God is somehow 'beyond' or 'outside' time, as if 'time' means nothing to him. Peter is biblical and not Greek in his thinking. He is not describing God as 'timeless and spaceless' as if we simply have to live with that. Peter's point is that God himself does not make plans that have to be fulfilled in a life-time, for he lives forever. Rather they will be fulfilled, and they will be fulfilled in history in time, but God views that time differently from us for whom it rushes by in a few short years (see the point made very clearly in Psalm 90:10).

The Lord is not slow in keeping his promise, as some understand slowness. This is the issue. God has promised a 'coming' (verse 4). Will he keep his word? Time and again Peter has returned to the issue of God and his word. It is active and powerful. What God says, happens. He can be trusted and will keep these promises of **the day of the Lord** (verse 10). As so often, Peter draws upon the Old Testament to make his point by alluding to Habakkuk 2:3 – 'For the revelation awaits an appointed time; it speaks of the end and will not prove false. Though it linger, wait for it; it will certainly come and will not delay.'

The fact that these promises may seem slow in coming to fruition has been interpreted by some to mean that they will not come to pass, that God is not really interested and has stood back. Such people should heed the words of the prophets and of Jesus (see next verse), and now of the apostle Peter.

Peter is prepared to admit that there is a delay but it must

be understood altogether differently, he argues. It all has to
do with God's grace and love for people. **He is patient with
you...** This is how the delay should be viewed, from the
perspective of God's patience as he provides still further time
for repentance **... not wanting any to perish, but everyone
to come to repentance**.

It is possible that Peter was here referring to God's desire
to see all people everywhere in the world repent. This is what
Paul refers to in 1 Timothy 2:3-4 when he urges prayer for
everyone and specially rulers because 'This is good, and
pleases God our Saviour, who wants all men to be saved and
to come to a knowledge of the truth'. The fact that *not* all are
saved or come to a knowledge of the truth indicates that we
are not here dealing with a *decree* of God nor even a promise,
for he always carries out that type of *will*. Rather Paul is
summarising the *desire* of God. It is his desire to see all people
obey the command to repent but he has not decreed that all
shall do this. But is this really what Peter has in mind here in
verse 9?

While it is possible Peter is thinking along these lines, it
does not quite do justice to what he actually writes. Peter
specifically addresses **you**. He says, 'He is patient **with you**.'
God is being patient while the believers come to repentance.
Now some commentators draw attention to this and suggest
that Peter is thus explaining the delay in terms of God's grace
to these believers who have perhaps followed the heretics
and now need to repent. God is giving them time to do so
before he comes in judgment. The **everyone** therefore refers
to all who are believers in *that* church. Personally, I do not
find this argument altogether convincing, though it does do
justice to the words of this verse. The problem with this
interpretation is that it doesn't actually provide an answer to
those who scoff. They are arguing that the delay has gone on
since the beginning! The Old Testament prophets foretold

the day of the Lord, but surely the delay cannot be explained simply in terms of this church that Peter is now dealing with! Even the believers were only too well aware that the delay had lasted much much longer than they had even been in existence as a church – that was just the point the false teachers were making as they scoffed and mocked the idea of the 'coming'.

Another alternative seems to make sense of the whole passage and take account of the specific wording of verse 9 that it is addressed to **you**. These people have to come to repentance. God doesn't want them to perish and he is giving time. He is patient with **you**, that is, with all who believe but also all who *will* believe. The whole purpose of this patience is that *all* God's people will come to repentance. Peter is addressing a particular group of God's people who have been given time and are being given time. Some have repented, some will repent and escape judgment, because they will listen to Peter's letter and, as the delay continues, so still more of God's people will come to repentance and find salvation.

In this day and age, the word comes to us across the ages because we are part of the people of God as believers and have benefited from that time of grace. Peter may have been addressing a particular group of people, but what he said was ultimately the answer to the question of the delay for all generations of believers. **He is patient with you** (his people), graciously waiting for your repentance. How good is our God!

Excursus: God and Time

It is worth pausing here for a moment to say a little more about God and time. Many, many Christians have argued that God must be 'timeless' and 'spaceless' and therefore to talk of time at all when we talk of God does not really make sense. His eternal nature, it is said, puts him in what we might call an eternal 'now'. He *is* in the past, present and future, but even such suggestions are at best human attempts to describe God.

We need to be very careful here, however. Certain principles should guide us in all our talk about God.

i) We must recognise that we can never fully describe God in any of his attributes let alone in his eternity.

ii) We should only seek to describe God to the extent that Scriptures give us genuine encouragement to do so and the means of doing so. In other words our God-language should be *biblical* language.

iii) We should be careful about making too many 'logical deductions' from truths that *are* revealed about God in Scripture so that we then move to teaching as certainties about God things that are actually not discussed or not revealed in Scripture.

Having said this, the Bible urges us to recognise God as eternal. His eternity is at the heart of much biblical worship and praise. He pre-existed the creation. His word brought into being all that we know in this world. His plans and purposes for mankind were laid out before the foundation of the earth and we know at least some of what the future holds because it has been laid out for us in the Scriptures, like these in 2 Peter that we are now examining. We also know that God is entirely free to do as he wishes. He is not contingent upon anything or anyone. He cannot therefore be said to be 'bound' by time as we know it, and surely Scripture gives us ample ground for understanding that he is greater than, and not bound by, what we would now call the universe (space).

However, we can only describe God in ways that make sense to us as his creation, and we should be governed by what he says to us. He has created us to understand time and to be bound by it. He has created us to understand at least something of our universe and of space and to be bound by it. We do not have to leave time or space to encounter God. We do not have to move into some other 'spiritual' world or the place of the 'gods' to find him. He has revealed himself to us *within* time and space. The whole of Scripture reveals God to us in terms of linear time. *For God himself,* there was a time *before* the beginning of our world, there is the time in which this world exists, and a time *in the future* when a new heaven and a new earth will exist. There was a time *before* God came to this earth in human form, and therefore a time, as far as this has been revealed to us, *before which* Jesus did exist but *not* in human form. From his birth onwards Jesus existed also as a man and now exists as a resurrected human being for all eternity. The earth goes on until, one day, God *will* bring it to an end, after which those who are judged will suffer *eternal* punishment and those who have been forgiven will enjoy *eternal* joy in the presence of God.

While all this may sound rather theoretical, we need to realise that if we do not describe God in the way he has revealed himself to us, we can easily say too much or too little and thus create a God after our own image. This will always be our temptation. Greek philosophical explanations about God and time run so deeply through western learning and culture that we are always tempted to discuss God in those terms. We would be much better thanking God that he has chosen to reveal himself to us within the confines of time, which he created for us to live in. We would be much better not speculating about whether he does or could exist outside of time or space, for we only know him within both.

But the day of the Lord will come like a thief. The heavens will disappear with a roar; the elements will be destroyed by fire, and the earth and everything in it will be laid bare (verse 10).

Patience with his people is one thing, but Peter wants his readers to be sure that, no matter how long the delay, such patience is not forever. God's people must repent and prepare themselves. Drawing directly upon the teaching of Jesus himself, Peter emphatically insists that **the day of the Lord** (the final judgment day and return of Christ) **will come.**[41] The temptation for all Christians over the centuries is to live as if the world will simply go on and on as it has since the beginning. They may not deny the 'Coming' as the false teachers do, but their lives do not reflect a belief that Christ will return. So Peter insists that the coming will be **like a thief**. He had used the prophet Habakkuk to explain the delay, now he draws upon the teaching of Jesus to warn that, delay or not, the outcome is certain.

In Matthew 24:43-44 Jesus had warned that if a house owner had known what time the thief would come he would have made preparations! 'So you also must be ready, because the Son of Man will come at an hour when you do not expect him.' In 1 Thessalonians, a letter that Peter's audience may well have known (see 2 Peter 3:15), the apostle Paul drew on the same teaching. In 1 Thessalonians 5:1-2 we read: 'you know very well that the day of the Lord will come like a thief in the night.' Thieves do not give advance notice of their intentions to raid a house, and this is how it will be with the day of the Lord. There is general advance notice. It *will* happen, but the specific time is not known so we should prepare properly.

When Christ returns **The heavens will disappear** (Greek 'pass away') with a roar. Peter has been drawing on Jesus'

---

41. 'Will come' is placed for emphasis right at the start of the Greek sentence.

words in Matthew 24 and there we also read in verse 35 that
'heaven and earth will pass away'. The **roar** vividly depicts
the consuming fire to which Peter now returns (see comments
on verse 7). **the elements will be destroyed by fire** is clear
in its general meaning that everything will be destroyed, but
what specifically does Peter mean by using the word we
translate as 'elements'? He may have in mind the old idea of
the elements of earth, wind and fire, or else the stars, planets
and other objects in the universe. Given that he has specifically
referred here to **the heavens** disappearing, we can reasonably
assume that the **elements** that **will be destroyed** consist of
all that we might describe as 'out there' in space.

Together with that destruction of our whole universe Peter
continues, **the earth and everything in it will be laid bare.**[42]
All that men and women have struggled to build and create
over the years will simply be exposed to God's searing
judgment.

Special Lessons for Today

Peter does not accept the mechanistic view of the universe
put forward by the false teachers and so prevalent today. From
a Christian perspective the world simply does not go on for
ever the same. God is at work in this world. He created it and
will bring it to an end. It has not simply come into being by
chance nor will it simply disappear by chance or even by the
will of a human being, say, through releasing a nuclear bomb
and starting a war that affects the whole world. Such a world
view is ultimately fatalistic. Many believers have, at least
emotionally, bought into that fatalism. Peter urges us to
remember God's activity. He is in sovereign control of all
that goes on and will, in his own time, cause the world to

---

42. There is widespread debate among scholars concerning the original word
used in the Greek. There are a number of textual variants. The one the New
International Version opts for is reasonably likely and literally means 'will
be found'.

come to an end, and create a new heaven and a new earth for
forgiven sinners to enjoy.

e) Therefore live holy and godly lives (verses 11-16)

**Since everything will be destroyed in this way, what kind of
people ought you to be? You ought to live holy and godly lives
as you look forward to the day of God and speed its coming**
(verses 11-12a).

The theme of destruction really began in this epistle back in
2:1 where the 'destructive' doctrines of the false teachers
would lead to their 'destruction'. The same point is made
again in 2:3. In 3:6-7 Peter went on to talk of the example of
the destruction of the world of Noah's day as judgment on
godless people. There he introduced the theme that he has
developed in verse 10. But now he moves on to draw
conclusions, **Since everything will be destroyed**[43]... What
about us? What about those who belong to God and *have*
repented? What about the faithful who await this return of
the Lord? Peter maintains that there should be two altogether
positive responses to belief in the day of the Lord and Christ's
return.

i) *Godly lives.* The first and most important, specially in
the light of the moral corruption of the heretics, is that true
believers must lead godly lives – **You ought to live holy
and godly lives**. This command recurs throughout Scripture.
The right response to the promises and works of God is, as
the apostle Paul put it in Romans 12:1, to offer our 'bodies as
living sacrifices, holy and pleasing to God'. Holy and godly
lives are those that are dedicated to God in every area. In
other words the Christian's life is to conform morally in all

---

43. Although in the Greek a different word is now used in verses 10-12, the
New International Version rightly continues to speak of 'destroyed and
'destruction'. The Revised Standard Version and others here translate the
verb *lyo* as 'dissolve'. The different Greek verbs are *apolyo* and *lyo*.

his or her thinking and works, to the will of God. This insistence on holiness as the right response to God is a prominent theme in 1 Peter as well. There, in 1:15-16 we read: 'Just as he who called you is holy, so be holy in all you do; for it is written: "Be holy, because I am holy" ' (quoting Leviticus 11:45). Such lives will offer a direct contrast with the heretics who are 'slaves of depravity' (2:19) as they continue in their 'shameful ways' (2:2).

As Christians seek to live this godly and holy life, they must remember the great encouragement found in Peter's opening verses of this letter, specially verse 3 (see the comments on that verse), where he reminded them, 'His divine power has given us everything we need for life and godliness through our knowledge of him who called us by his own glory and goodness.' God has not left Christians to battle on on their own, but enables them to fulfil this demand and so receive still further encouragement as they look forward to Christ's return. This leads us into Peter's second point.

ii) *Joyful anticipation*. The second response must be one of joyful expectation and anticipation of the fulfilment of God's promises. **As you look forward to the day of God** captures this sense of waiting but also looking forward – **and speed its coming**. Christians need never fear the coming of Christ. For all the talk of destruction and judgment, the Christian can look forward to that day without fear because, through repentance and faith in Christ, he or she can be assured of salvation from such horrors (verse 15). Indeed, as God's people come to faith, repent and move on to lead holy and godly lives so, from our human point of view, we are reducing the length of time he needs to be patient (verse 9). If the delay in Christ's coming is due to God's grace as he waits for his people to repent, then their repentance, reflected in their lives, speeds the return of Christ.

Of course, we need to be careful here. Peter is not implying

that Christ's return is dependent on the people of God coming
to repentance. The 'coming' is entirely in the sovereign hands
of the heavenly Father but still, from our perspective,
repentance and godly lives among God's people should
provide us with an even greater reason for having a lively
and confident expectation that this return may be at any time.

> **That day will bring about the destruction of the heavens by
> fire, and the elements will melt in the heat. But in keeping
> with his promise we are looking forward to a new heaven and
> a new earth, the home of righteousness** (verses 12b-13).

Peter now summarises in two brief sentences what he is
saying. The promise of God to judge on the day of God has
not failed as the heretics have maintained, for the destruction
will indeed take place. However, neither has the most
wonderful promise of God of a new heaven and a new earth
failed. Just as surely as destruction will happen, so those who
belong to God can be assured, **in keeping with his promise,**[44]
that he will create **a new heaven and a new earth**. Just as
the prophets and specially, as we saw earlier, Isaiah, had
promised the conflagration of the wicked (see comments on
verse 7), so they had promised comfort to the godly. In Isaiah
66:22 we read: ' "As the new heavens and the new earth that
I make will endure before me," declares the LORD, "so will
your name and descendents endure." ' This too is God's
promise. This too is among the promises which the heretics
have scorned, yet this is what must provide the joy and
anticipation that should be felt by all God's people as they
await the day of the Lord.

They await **the home of righteousness**. This wonderful
description of the new heaven and the new earth says it all.
This is what things will be like when God has taken decisive
action on the final day. There will be no more evil, or

---

44. See comments on 1:4 regarding the 'precious promises'.

temptation to follow the corrupt desires of a sinful nature, for we shall find instead a place 'in which righteousness lives'.

Special Lessons for Today

There is so much we should apply to our own lives here, but let me draw attention to three areas of great importance.

i) *The call to holiness and godliness.* We have noted this before in this epistle, but as Peter returns to it so should we, again and again. Too often we find all sorts of excuses for what should simply be regarded as 'ungodly' behaviour. The very word 'holy' implies being marked out or 'set apart'. We should be noticeably different in our life-style and behaviour and in our priorities from those around who do not believe in Christ and have not repented. If we are not in fact seen to be different, if we do not feel like 'aliens and strangers in the world' (1 Peter 2:11), then we are disregarding the word of God and failing to be the witnesses to his light and his righteousness that we should be. In many churches nowadays there is little emphasis on godliness and holiness. All the thrust of teaching seems to be towards how God may help us to 'feel' better, or the way God may 'heal' us. Such teaching is not improper, but the balance is all wrong. Our response to God's work of salvation in our lives should be seen immediately in godly and holy lives, now lived for God rather than for ourselves.

ii) *Being ready for the return.* There is a direct relationship between the lack of teaching about holiness and godliness and the lack of teaching that we should be ready for Christ's imminent return. In this letter from Peter the two teachings go hand in hand. If we truly believe that Christ might return tomorrow, that the world will be destroyed by fire and only those who belong to God will be saved, then surely we should seek to live lives that clearly evidence the fact that we belong to God. It seems to me that the church often gets this teaching

about Christ's return wrong in two very different ways at the
moment. There are those who rarely if ever talk of Christ's
return to judge. In such circles it is almost not 'politically
correct' to mention such things! We are told we must only
talk of God's love and not of his justice, and so on. This has
led to a weak and insipid church with no real gospel of
salvation to preach. False teachers are unlikely to be
recognised in such circles unless they are totally outlandish!
But at the other end of the spectrum are those who spend so
much time discussing the detail of when and how the Lord
will return and whether this sign or that sign has yet been
seen, that they are in danger of forgetting Peter's point that a
thousand years in the Lord's sight are like a day. We are to
have a perspective on these matters which reflects the patient
grace of God. While the return of Christ is a vital doctrine
for our lives, and one of the most 'precious promises' in
Scripture, it should produce Christians who are most eager
to be holy and godly and who are most eager to evangelise
while there is still time. Such Christians have a much deeper
grasp of the meaning of Christ's return than those who spend
vast amounts of time discussing the detail and seeming to
forget that, at the end of the day, only God the Father knows
when that day will be.

iii) *Optimism about the future*. There are many reasons to
feel despondent about our world, as there have been in every
age. But the Christian should not be driven by pessimism,
but by a firm optimism. The sovereign Lord is in control.
This is an age of grace for God's people, so let's make use of
it as we call men and women to respond to the Good News of
salvation. Let us also relax in the knowledge that one day we
shall enjoy the new heaven and the new earth and live there
in the presence of God, in the home of righteousness.[45] How
sad it is to see so many Christians speaking about this world

---

45. See 'Appendix: New Heaven, New Body', pp. 137-142.

in ways that are little better than the ways a fatalist might speak. We know the Lord of creation, the God of eternity, the Saviour, and so we can rest assured that our world is in his hands even while we eagerly anticipate his 'coming'.

So then, dear friends, since you are looking forward to this, make every effort to be found spotless, blameless and at peace with him (verse 14).

Peter again appeals to these 'much loved' people who are in so much danger of being led astray. They are to look forward to (literally) 'these things', that is, the new heaven and new earth and all that accompanies the day of the Lord, and therefore should make every endeavour to lead the holy and godly lives of which he has been talking. Here, however, he uses words drawn from the Old Testament sacrificial background. We are reminded of the sacrificial lamb that was to be without 'spot or blemish' (e.g. Leviticus 1:3; 'without defect' – NIV). Such an offering is acceptable to God and is befitting worship of God. But that reminder is probably only indirectly what Peter has in mind. It is more likely that Peter is remembering Jesus, the perfect sacrifice and the perfect example for us to follow. In 1 Peter 1:19 the apostle recalls that we were redeemed by the 'precious blood of Christ, a lamb without blemish or defect'. What a difference there will be between these followers of Christ and the heretics who 'are blots and blemishes' in the church (see comments on 2:13).

Not only should a Christian be found on that last day to be Christ-like but also he should be found **at peace with him**. Peter is not simply talking about peaceful and contented feelings about our relationship with God. Rather it has to do with *not* being God's enemies, not being among those who will be judged by him. The apostle Paul expounds upon this point at length in Romans 5 where he compares our having been 'enemies of God' (Romans 5:10) with now being 'at peace with him' through justification (5:1).

> **Bear in mind that our Lord's patience means salvation, just as our dear brother Paul also wrote to you with the wisdom that God gave him** (verse 15).

Being at peace with God sums up the end result of the gospel of salvation. As Christians reflect on this while looking forward to Christ's coming, they should specially **bear in mind** that the delay in his return (**our Lord's patience**) has meant that they have had time to be saved and to find peace with God. See the comments on his 'patience' in verse 9 above.

f) Some comments on Paul and Scripture (verses 15-16)

The apostle Paul had made the same point to them, says Peter, acknowledging the **wisdom God gave him**. By this Peter affirms, no doubt, Paul's apostolic authority as God **gave** him the wisdom for what he said and wrote. Why Peter should appeal to Paul at this point has been a matter of considerable debate. Some have suggested that it shows the apostle Peter could not have written this letter, else he would not have needed to appeal to any other apostle. However, two simple solutions suggest themselves. The first is that Peter knows his letter is closely following on one written by Paul, perhaps a year or two or even only a few months earlier. We have no knowledge of this, but it could offer a very simple explanation of Peter's reference to Paul and a letter he knew they had already received. More likely is that this is yet another instance in which Peter is seeking to show that the promises of God are to be found in the prophets, and from Jesus through the apostles. Peter will go on to talk of Paul's writing as 'Scripture'. Peter, the apostle, is saying that his teaching about the future and judgment and the Lord's coming and his divine patience are all to be found in other authoritative apostolic teachings like those of Paul. Indeed almost all of the writings of the apostle Paul known to us in Scripture talk at some length about Christ's return. And that is just what Peter goes on to say.

He writes the same way in all his letters, speaking in them of these matters (verse 16a). We do not know with how many of Paul's letters Peter was acquainted. What is quite fascinating here is that it is very early evidence that already at least Paul's apostolic letters were being collected together and being given a wider circulation than their original audience. Clearly, as we shall see later in this verse, the letters were being accorded the status of Scripture. Some have used this fact as an argument for a very late date for 2 Peter, long after the apostle's death. But there is no need to assume this at all. Peter and Paul probably both died under the Neronic persecutions in Rome in the 60s. There is no reason why Peter could not have seen some of Paul's letters which were perhaps being read in the churches in Rome.

His letters contain some things that are hard to understand, which ignorant and unstable people distort, as they do the other Scriptures, to their own destruction (verse 16b).

I have known students of the New Testament who have been tempted to use this verse to excuse their lack of diligence in the study of Paul's epistles! But Peter is not saying that Paul's writings *cannot* be understood. He only says that **some things are hard to understand**, and perhaps he specially has in mind some of his teaching about the future and the return of the Lord. Peter's is not at all a counsel of despair for those of us who would like to come to grips with Paul's writings! Rather we should note that some of those 'hard' passages are distorted by **ignorant and unstable people**. Presumably Peter has in mind the false teachers who, he is arguing, have deliberately (see verse 5) forgotten and distorted and ignored those parts of Scripture that do not suit them. If a passage is generally hard to understand it may more easily be used by such people in a distorted way. Gullible people who cannot easily understand certain Scriptures may too easily be convinced that a false teacher is right in his interpretation.

Peter then adds, **as they do the other Scriptures**. In other words, a characteristic trait of these false teachers is that they distort and twist Scripture around to suit their own views and teachings. For those who wonder whether their own church leaders can be trusted in what they are teaching or whether they may be in danger of being led astray, the way Scripture is treated is one of the best tests. Ask yourself whether your minister or housegroup/cell group teacher ignores some Scripture, or dismisses some Scriptures as 'irrelevant', or perhaps refuses to answer questions about his or her interpretation of certain Scriptures. Ask yourself whether what you hear from the pulpit is an exposition of Scripture or a series of relatively pious sounding thoughts and cleverly rehearsed anecdotes that have no foundation in the Word of God.

What is fascinating about Peter's comments here is that he links Paul's writing to 'Scriptures'. The word **other** is deeply significant. The Greek word translated as 'Scriptures' here is only used in the New Testament to describe the authoritative teaching of God in the Old Testament. Now Peter links to those foundational and Spirit-inspired writings the work of the apostle Paul. This is one of the very earliest examples we have of writings that we know in the New Testament being regarded as fully inspired of the Holy Spirit and counted as being as authoritative as the Old Testament. Of course, at this stage it was not in any sense a 'New Testament canon', but nevertheless it indicates the tremendous authority and level of inspiration by the Holy Spirit which was assumed to be true of apostolic writings.

Twisting and distorting the Bible may not seem particularly serious, but here Peter shows us just how serious it is. Distorting the Old Testament, the words and promises of Jesus, and the teachings of the apostles leads these false teachers **to their own destruction**. Peter has referred many times to this destruction. It is a most serious statement for all generations of those who claim to be Christians. Deliberate distortion, manipulation or 'forgetting' of Scripture is at the heart of this false teaching. God's Word might be hard to understand in places, but that is no excuse. Scripture can be weighed against Scripture, Peter can be used to help us understand aspects of teaching that may be difficult elsewhere and so on, but deliberate distortion of the Word of God leads to destruction.

Special Lessons for Today

We have already noted how important it is to trust in the Scriptures (see final comments on chapter 1). But Peter drives us back to this again here in chapter 3. We must heed the whole of what Peter is saying here. First, he is saying that true Christians need to be building their lives upon the promises of God and he has specially in mind the promises of judgment and of salvation. They will therefore be seeking to lead lives that are without spot or blemish – Christ-like lives. But secondly, he is saying that those promises are to be believed because they are part of Scripture, the received Word of God.

Distortion of any part of the promises and commands of God in Scripture leads to destruction. How important it is that we sit up and take note of this! First, we must do so for ourselves. This is not simply a question of having a right 'doctrine of Scripture'. It is not just a matter of believing Scripture to be trustworthy, but, as Peter has urged upon his readers, it is a matter of obedience to *the whole of Scripture* that is important. A godly and holy life will provide at least a partial indication of whether a person or a leader is treating Scripture as fully authoritative.

In this passage of 2 Peter we have also seen how the apostle weighs Scripture with Scripture. The Old Testament, the apostolic teaching and words of Christ are all brought together to understand the fullness of what God is speaking to us. If it is difficult to understand Peter or Paul, we are to look at the 'other' Scriptures. Here again is something that is often ignored in our day and age. Specially in Biblical studies there is a tendency to treat every book as completely separate from other Scriptures. People talk of 'Paul's theology', 'John's theology' and so on. Of course, we find different emphases between the writers, otherwise presumably God would not have given us a number of different writings from different authors to form the Scriptures. Nevertheless, Peter is committed to what we might call 'Biblical theology'. He expects Christians to look at different Scriptures in the Old Testament and in the New, as we now call them. Weighing Peter's words in the light of Paul's is just part of what he is saying. Peter has modelled for us, as do all the New Testament writers, the need to look at Scripture *as a whole* if we are to understand it properly. Where one passage is hard to understand, then it is right to seek understanding elsewhere in Scripture and to interpret Scripture in the light of Scripture. Peter understands a *unity* in Scripture that is often not seen in our age. Let us remember God has given us sixty-six books in the Bible for a reason. It is only in the whole that we have the full verbal revelation of God that he wants us to have.

7. Closing Remarks – (3:17-18)

Therefore, dear friends, since you already know this, be on your guard so that you may not be carried away by the error of lawless men and fall from your secure position. But grow in the grace and knowledge of our Lord and Saviour Jesus Christ. To him be glory both now and for ever! Amen (verses 17-18).

Therefore, dear friends draws the readers back to the challenges of verses 11-15. And so by way of summary, Peter makes his final appeal for action by saying **since you already know this**. That is, since they already know false teachers will come among them in the last days, both from apostolic teaching, from this letter from Peter, the words of Christ and even the Old Testament prophets (see specially 3:2), they should take appropriate defensive action. Of course, they also **already know this** because, as verse 16 has made clear, the ignorant and unstable are *already* distorting apostolic teaching even in Paul's and Peter's own life-time.

So Peter makes two final appeals, the first is more negative and defensive and recalls the call he had made in chapter 2 to beware of and recognise false teachers. The second appeal is more positive and urges Christians to go on the offensive, recalling some of the great encouragements seen in chapter 1.

a) Be on your guard (verse 17)

First, he says, you should recognise the false teachers for who they are and **be on your guard so that you may not be carried away by the error of lawless men and fall from your secure position**. As we have seen throughout the epistle, there is a need to recognise who the enemy is and that is done by being 'on guard' all the time so that true believers are not carried away into error. Peter has shown all sorts of ways in which believers should be on guard. They should watch out for immorality, for the distortion of Scripture, and beware lest they or others forget the promises of God. The dangers of being carried away by error are real enough.

Peter chooses his words carefully here in his summary. The word 'error', which comes from the root word 'to wander', reminds us of the false teachers who have 'wandered off' in 2:15. They are **lawless**, a word used in 2:7 to describe the people of Sodom! Reference to **your secure position** here recalls 1:12 where Peter had encouraged his readers by acknowledging that they 'are firmly established[46] in the truth'. His summary appeal here in verse 18, therefore, urges the Christians to remain established in the truth. Truth leads to standing firm before God while **error** leads to the **fall** before God on the judgment day (see 1:10-11). Peter's appeal is not unlike the apostle Paul's appeal in 1 Corinthians 10:12, 'So, if you think you are standing firm, be careful that you don't fall!'

b) Grow in grace (verse 18a)
Secondly, Peter says that they should **grow in the grace and knowledge of our Lord and Saviour Jesus Christ**. I once took a person through one of our courses which seeks to lay foundations for the Christian faith and help new Christians to grow in Christ. At the end of that course this man, who seemed to have become a real Christian, was asked whether he would like to study further, or what he was going to do now to continue growing in the faith. His response was something like this: 'Nothing! I am not an academic. I don't need to go on studying the faith or the Bible, as long as I love Jesus, that's all that matters.' In spite of much encouragement and urging on my part, this man never even joined a housegroup let alone another course. Gradually he dropped off church. For a while he began to attend another church,

---

46. The verb here in Greek is derived from the noun in 3:18 translated 'secure position'.

but he never became involved there either, and, as far as I am
aware, has never even tried to grow as a Christian. The result
is that today it appears he is nowhere spiritually. His
occasional attendances at church do little to suggest that he
has a healthy vibrant faith. Sadly in the modern church this is
a common story.

Part of this has to do with the age we live in. There is an
anti-intellectual climate around, specially in England. Study
is considered elitist and too much like hard work. But Peter
is not saying that you have to be highly educated in order to
grow in the **knowledge of our Lord**. Certainly, as he has
shown, Christians will want to read and learn from the whole
of the Bible. Certainly teaching and preaching from God's
word is one of the ways we grow in our knowledge of the
Lord. But let us not allow Bible study to be regarded as an
'intellectual study'. God will use our intellects to whatever
depth he has given us such abilities, but growing in the way
Peter now describes is not simply an intellectual exercise. It
is about listening to God's word, grasping his promises and
his commands, and then seeking to live out that truth. Often
it is the least intellectual members of a church who will put
to shame the academics in our midst. Because they have
grown further than others, they have grown to see that they
must live by what they have been taught.

It is important to see that Peter puts **grace** before
knowledge. In many religions knowledge becomes the key
to accessing God. In the Christian faith, the fact of the matter
is that not only do we come to know God in the first place by
his grace, but that all subsequent growth is also part of his
continuing gracious activity in our lives. This takes us right
back to the start of Peter's letter (specially 1:2-4). The
believers to whom Peter writes, like all Christians, have come
to faith by God's gracious work in their lives. However,
coming to faith is only the first stage in a life-long path to

spiritual maturity. Peter has already explained much of what
is involved with this growing in grace, specially in 1:5-11.
But the means for this growth has been given us graciously
by 'his divine power' (1:3). As we grow, so we find God at
work within us, conforming us more and more to the likeness
of Jesus himself.

and knowledge of our Lord and Saviour Jesus Christ.
Is this **knowledge** of Jesus speaking of our personal
relationship with him, as in 1:2? Or is this **knowledge**
something given to us by Jesus, like the **grace** already
mentioned? It may really be both,[47] but the former is more
likely in this context. The wonderful final appeal Peter is
making urges growth, for which we have the continuing grace
of the Lord, and thus urges an even deeper relationship with[48]
(knowledge of) Christ.

How we should all long for that deeper knowledge of and
relationship with Jesus! Herein lies our Christian joy, but
here also lies our ultimate defence against false teachers.
Through his grace, through the relationship the Lord Jesus
forges with us, his children, we will not fall from our secure
position (3:17) but will remain firmly established in the truth'
(1:12).

c) To Christ be glory (verse 18b)

Just as Jesus 'called us by his own glory and goodness' (1:3),
so Peter now declares **To him be glory both now and for
ever! Amen**. As we saw in the comments on 1:3, **glory**
expresses the divinity of Jesus. Peter thus ascribes worship
to Jesus as God, much as he opened his epistle by reference
to 'our God and Saviour Jesus Christ'.

The Christian's faith begins and ends with the grace of
Jesus Christ, the **Saviour**. The Saviour 'saved' his people
from the judgment of God by taking that judgment on himself

---

47. See comments on 1:2.   48. Again see comments on 1:2.

as he died on the cross. He calls people to himself, forgives them, and continues to uphold them so they stand firm. Undoubtedly, he is to be worshipped from the depths of our being, **both now and for ever**[49], for all eternity.

Thus Peter concludes this wonderful and highly relevant epistle. He begins and ends with the grace of the Lord Jesus and his great glory. But he also calls on all believers to trust in God's promises and his word. Christ will return whatever false teachers may say. Christians, therefore, must be able to recognise false prophets and teachers and see the bankruptcy of what they teach. Rather than following them into sin, Christians must lead holy and godly lives in the grace and power provided by Christ himself. They must see their goal as growing in the grace of Christ and in an ever-deepening knowledge of, and relationship with, him.

The path described here by Peter is the path all who have faith in Christ must follow. In this way we will indeed be able to 'escape the corruption in the world caused by evil desires' and, instead, find that most wonderful of blessings – that we may 'participate in the divine nature' (1:4) and thus bring glory to his name.

Appendix: New Heaven, New Body
In 2 Peter 1:13-14 we noted how Peter could talk of the tent of this body and how he would soon put it aside. In common with Jesus and other New Testament writers, he believed in the final resurrection when he would be given a new body. In this last chapter of the epistle we have seen Peter's emphasis on the day of the Lord (3:10), and God's promise of a new heaven and a new earth (3:13). Peter does not go into detail about the type of body this resurrection body will be, nor does he describe

---

49. The Greek is perhaps better translated as 'both now and into the day of eternity', implying that Peter is thinking of our worship of him as it continues beyond his return, beyond 'the day of the Lord'.

the new heaven and earth. Nevertheless, there are some indications about both these matters elsewhere in Scripture.

i) *a resurrected body*.

In commenting on 1:13-14 we noted that Peter had seen the risen Lord Jesus and knew that a real, though different, body awaited him at the bodily resurrection. Peter and the other apostles knew something of the resurrected body because they had seen the risen Christ. It is mainly in the apostle Paul's writings that we receive a few indications of what the new body will be like. Paul's analogies in 1 Corinthians 15:35-44 indicate that we cannot be precise in our descriptions this side of the day of the Lord. But Paul reminds us that

a) *there will be continuity between old and new*. Just as there is continuity between the seed of corn which seems so small and dead and the full ear of corn that seems so alive and large and beautiful, so it will be between the bodies that believers have on this earth and the bodies they will have when raised from the dead.

b) *resurrected bodies will be glorious*. They will reflect the glory of God himself, as they 'shine like the sun' (Matthew 13:43). There will be a godly wonder and beauty about resurrected bodies as they reflect the same glory seen in the bodies of Moses and Elijah at the Transfiguration. The Transfiguration was a foretaste of the resurrection glory (see Luke 9:30-31).

c) *they will be spiritual bodies*. This does not at all mean 'non physical', as if the new body is somehow like a disembodied ghost or spirit. The contrast is between *natural* and *spiritual* (see 1 Corinthians 15:44). In this world our bodies follow the desires of this mode of existence with its preoccupations with self, in the new order our bodies will be subject fully to God's will and will be preoccupied with serving him.

d) *they will be imperishable*. The new body will be fit for the new order of things. What is temporary and passing will be left behind and what is permanent and glorious and unending and unfading replaces the old. These bodies will be ready for eternity where there will be no more death or mourning or crying or pain (Revelation 21:4).

We cannot know much else for certain about the resurrected body. As we look at Jesus' resurrection appearances we can see that his body was physical enough (as we understand the meaning) for him to be able to eat with his disciples and for him to be recognised (e.g. Luke 24:41-43), even his crucifixion scars were visible (John 20:26-27); and yet he was not always recognised until he chose to reveal himself (Luke 24:28-32). Ultimately, the Biblical evidence, though limited, makes it clear that the resurrected body is deliberately designed by God to live in the new heaven and new earth.

ii) *The new heaven and earth.*
Ever since the sin of Adam and Eve and their expulsion by God from the Garden of Eden, God has held before his people the prospect of a time when the judgment of death and exclusion would be reversed. Throughout the Old Testament the Israelites looked forward to the fulfilment of God's covenant promises. He promised them an inheritance of land, that he would be in their midst, that they would know peace from enemies and have long life in the land and enjoy rich blessings coming from the land's harvests. The land of Israel was to be the inherited land. The temple in Jerusalem was the place where God's glory lived among them. But even God's people continued to sin and to experience the on-going judgment of the Lord. Though they saw something of the potential of Israel, they never properly experienced a long period of peace. The rich blessings of the land were often

raided by others and finally they were conquered. Even the temple was torn down.

The prophets wrestled with the realities that God's people were facing: of promises apparently unfulfilled, of sin among the covenant people, and of the lack of joy and peace. God revealed to them that these promises were not forgotten. In various ways he pointed them forward to a time of salvation, to a future king like David who would rule forever and to a kingdom of peace and righteousness (e.g. Isaiah 11; Jeremiah 23:4-8). He pointed forward to a place where God would indeed be among his people as had been expected of the temple in Jerusalem, and he pointed forward to a kingdom that would have many similarities with the Garden of Eden in its beauty and harvests.

In the latter chapters of Isaiah some of these strands of prophecy are specially prominent. In Isaiah 65 Isaiah looks forward to God's day of judgment and of salvation. Those who have sinned and rebelled will be judged, but salvation will come to God's faithful people. In verses 13-16 the faithful are contrasted with the others. Those who trust in God will come to that day and receive blessings. They will eat and be joyful. They will be given a new name and sing for joy, and 'past troubles will be forgotten'. Then in verse 17 more detail is put on this time in the future. Suddenly we are lifted beyond Israel and the possibility that one day the land will provide all they need and battles will be over. Instead: ' "Behold, I will create new heavens and a new earth. The former things will not be remembered, nor will they come to mind. But be glad and rejoice for ever in what I will create, for I will create Jerusalem to be a delight ... the sound of weeping and of crying will be heard in it no more." ' As the chapter continues, the picture of a perfected Jerusalem and God's presence therefore being among his people is combined with ideas that come from the Garden of Eden as we read, 'They will not toil in vain or bear children doomed to misfortune ... the wolf and the lamb will feed together...'

It is this understanding of the future that is picked up again in places in the New Testament, specially in 2 Peter 3 as we have seen, but also in Revelation 21:1: 'Then I saw a new heaven and a new earth.... I saw the Holy City, the new Jerusalem ... and God himself will be with them and be their God. He will wipe every tear from their eyes. There will be no more death or mourning or crying or pain, for the old order of things has passed away.' Then in chapter 22 we read 'no longer will there be any curse', and we see that in the new heaven and the new earth the Garden of Eden is, as it were, restored. Yet now it seems even better than the original, for Christ is in its midst, and so God reveals that, as it were, Jerusalem and the Garden of Eden are combined in what is new to provide the perfect inheritance so long anticipated by God's people.

The prospect is truly amazing. In keeping with his promise we are looking forward to all this (2 Peter 3:13). In that new earth, God's people, confirmed in righteousness and peace, will work in a way that fulfils the will of God for them. They will worship and enjoy the Lord for ever, for the new heaven and the new earth are permanent, and God's people will be prepared with suitable bodies for this eternal kingdom. Sue Read's hymn[50] captures something of the glory of the Biblical promises and our eager longing for their fulfilment.

When he comes his reign shall bring peace,
When he comes all fighting shall cease.
Men shall hammer their spears into pruning hooks
And prepare for battle no more.
When he comes, when he comes.
And on that day there will be laughter,

50. Sue Read. Hymn copyright Thankyou Music 1985.

On that day joy ever after,
No more tears for the Lord will wipe them all away
And on that day, men shall be brothers,
Reconciled to God and each other,
The world shall see the King in his glory,
When he comes.
When he comes, he'll be of David's line,
The mighty God and ruler divine.
They'll call him wonderful and Counsellor,
And his kingdom shall never cease.
When he comes, when he comes. –

JUDE

Introduction

Some years ago in our church I announced that I would be preaching on the book of Jude. Someone came up to me and asked what on earth I could get out of the book that would be of any use to anyone! There was a tone of exasperation in her voice. Perhaps I should not have been surprised. After all, for many Christians, the book of Jude is 'that little book that comes before Revelation'. Some people, if pushed, could remember the beautiful doxology from the last couple of verses. Others, like the one who approached me that Sunday, could remember that this was the book that talked about 'nether gloom', angels in chains and someone called Enoch. At first glance it must be admitted that Jude seems rather remote from life at the turn of the twenty-first century.

Relevance for today

Indeed, I have to confess that when I first started to read Jude and to prepare for preaching it, I did so more from a sense of duty than from some insight into the letter's important contribution to the life of the modern church. It was one of those occasions where my commitment to a belief that '*all* Scripture is inspired by God and profitable ...' caused me to look more carefully at a part of the Bible that I might otherwise have avoided. How exciting it was, then, to discover that this little book has much to say that is of real relevance and profit for the modern church.

It speaks of how God keeps and protects and cares for his people even when they are facing heresy. It exhorts Christians to contend earnestly for their faith, specially in the face of false teaching by godless and immoral people. Jude asks his readers to learn from history. Though the examples he uses do not immediately ring bells with people these days, once understood, their application is immediately apparent. Jude also tells Christians about the precautions they should take to prevent themselves being seduced away from the truth. He even suggests ways in which the godless teachers might be saved from judgment. Then, underlying the whole letter, is Jude's great commitment to the sovereignty of God.

God loves his people whom he keeps and who experience his mercy, peace and love. In spite of many different attacks upon his people, it is ultimately God himself who continues to prevent his people from falling. It is he alone, 'the only God our Saviour ... through Jesus Christ our Lord', who will indeed save for he has all 'glory, majesty, power and authority' for all eternity (verse 25).

The more I studied, the more I realised what I had been missing. In the end I preached several sermons, but more could have been said, for the truths of this epistle must be applied in a modern way to our own world and church. More than ever we know the problems of false teachers, of those who pervert the grace of God and act immorally yet claim to have faith, and more than ever we need to hear again the truth that we are part of *God's* church and it is he who keeps us and loves us and in his gracious sovereignty will bring his church to glory. But we also need to know what precautions we must take to defend ourselves against 'these people', as Jude calls them, and we need to be made aware of how best to help our friends as we see them being seduced by such false teaching and pagan life-styles.

The relationship between Jude and 2 Peter[1]

Anyone asked to write a commentary on Jude, as I have been asked to do, is invariably asked to write a commentary as well on the epistle of 2 Peter. At first glance this may seem

1. This section and other references to the relationship between the two epistles present essentially the same discussion as the similar sections in the commentary on 2 Peter. They are repeated here in order to enable the commentary on Jude to stand on its own, for those who do not wish to study 2 Peter at the same time.

strange. Why should commentaries on Jude and 2 Peter often be bound together? The answer to this is not easy but is best explained by comparing Jude with 2 Peter 2. The similarities between them are obvious even on a superficial reading. This relationship has been explained in a variety of ways. Generally it falls into three categories: a) Peter borrowed from Jude; b) Jude borrowed from Peter; c) both used a similar or the same source material.

Jude is only twenty-five verses long and fifteen of these appear in at least a very similar form in 2 Peter 2. It is impossible to be absolutely certain who actually wrote first. Some have suggested that if Peter borrowed from Jude (as 'a' above), apostolic authorship of 2 Peter is unlikely. It is suggested that an apostle would not have drawn on a minor figure like Jude. But this argument is far-fetched. Firstly, as we shall see, Jude was also regarded as having apostolic authority; and secondly, as many have pointed out, literature is full of examples of great writers who have borrowed from those less well-known than themselves.

The reasons some say Jude drew on 2 Peter (as 'b' above) can seem plausible enough but both 'a' and 'b' face problems. For example, it is said that

a) Peter often talks about the false teachers in the future tense, while Jude already views them as present. Some even suggest that Jude 17-18 looks back to 2 Peter 3:2,3. Yet, the fact is that Peter does not always use the future tense of these heretics.

b) Jude is more polished in its structure than is 2 Peter, and this may indicate a careful and reflective re-working of Peter's material. However, it may also mean that Peter simply remembered Jude's work and re-wrote it in a more relaxed way.

c) It is also often asked why Jude should have bothered to re-write 2 Peter in such a very short letter, while adding a minimum of his own ideas. However, Jude himself tells us that he writes with a certain urgency (Jude 3) and 'to remind you'. So perhaps he found Peter's letter to be the most useful message to pass on (again?) to the congregation.

My own view is that probably Jude and 2 Peter were written around the same time, but I am unpersuaded by any of the arguments supporting either those who believe Jude was written first or those who believe 2 Peter was written first.

Certainly the arguments about who came first and who borrowed from whom and the similarities of the epistles have clouded much of the teaching we find in *both* epistles. Similarities there are, and this may suggest either that they used a common source for some of their material and/or that some of the false teaching in both churches was similar. Nevertheless, the differences between the epistles are considerable as well. 2 Peter contains more in it that is *not* found in Jude than is found there. Jude tackles some different themes and so we must never be tempted to assume that if we have studied 2 Peter we can virtually ignore this book of Jude.

A largely Jewish audience

As we read Jude it will become clear that Jude and his audience had a good knowledge of Jewish teaching and traditions. Jude knew the Hebrew version of the Old Testament as well as the Greek translation and was able to make his own translations.[2] Jude writes in a 'Jewish' way. He makes his points by referring to a biblical text or story and then expounding it. This style would be most suitable if the people he was writing to came from a Palestinian Jewish background.

References to the angels, Michael, Satan, and a pre-occupation with the relationship between events in heaven

---

2. This reliance in some places upon the Hebrew version is most easily seen in the way he alludes to or uses the the Old Testament in his writing. For example, on occasion he gives his own translation which is not dependent upon the LXX (e.g. compare verse 12 with Proverbs 25:14; also verse 13 with Isaiah 57:20).

and events on earth, all of which can sound somewhat strange to our ears, would have been common-place in early Palestinian Jewish Christianity. In using these ideas in his teaching, Jude is following Jewish prophetic and 'apocalyptic' traditions.

Just where these Christians to whom Jude was writing lived is an open question, though from the above we may be right to assume the church was made up largely of converted Jews. However, given the way outside false teachers had managed to gain entrance, they probably found themselves living among pagans. Some commentators have plausibly suggested the recipients may have been a church in Syria, but because Jude tells us so little, we cannot be certain of this.

As we begin studying this book, there are, of course, other important questions which need to be asked such as who this Jude was, and when he wrote. But the best place to try and answer these is as we look at the text itself.

Overview of Jude's letter

Jude writes to a Christian community. He was going to write to them about **the salvation we share** (verse 3), but something intervened to make him change the content of his letter. We do not know what that was, but from what Jude goes on to say, perhaps he had just received news from the church which disturbed him. Verse 4 spells out the problem Jude felt needed urgent attention. **Certain ... godless men ... have secretly slipped in among you**. These people were immoral and denied Jesus Christ as Lord.

Bad theology and practice

The urgency of this situation ought to be obvious, but Jude drives it home by asking his readers to remember just how serious bad theology and practice can be in the life of God's people. He produces three warnings from the Old Testament (verses 5-7). In each of these examples, the groups had known something of the truth of God's grace but had perverted that grace and were subsequently judged by God.

In verses 8-13 Jude points out that both these false teachers and any who follow them will face the same judgment. The church needs to be aware of just how godless they are and how imminent their judgment may be.

The problems are not unexpected, so be prepared

Jude goes on to point out that the problem of false teaching is something for which the early church should be prepared. In the Jewish context they had only to think of the Book of Enoch with its dire warnings (verses 14-16). They also had the warnings of the apostles themselves which they should have heeded (verses 17-19).

Jude then follows the practice of most good preachers and applies what he has said directly to this church in verses 17-23. The prophetic warnings mean they should be *prepared*. They must make sure they do not fall prey to these insurgents. Protection lies in being well-founded in their faith, praying regularly, building themselves up in the faith, and keeping themselves in the love of God. Not only should they look after themselves spiritually, but they should consider how best to win back any who may have followed the immoral ways of these false teachers.

Yet God is sovereign

Ultimately, though, Jude is insistent that God is in control. Those whom he addressed as **called ... loved ... and kept by Jesus Christ** (verse 1) will indeed be kept from falling by our God and Saviour. The goal of the Christian life is to be brought into the glorious presence of God. Christians **wait for the mercy of our Lord Jesus Christ to bring** [them] **to eternal life** (verse 21), but it is God himself who will bring this about as he presents them **without fault and with great joy** before him in his own presence. Clearly there is great urgency to deal with a very serious problem, but Jude knows that the ultimate power and authority to protect God's people lies with God himself and that he will do just that through all eternity (verse 25).

An Outline of the Commentary

1.   Greetings from Jude (verses 1-2)

Jude, a servant of Jesus Christ and a brother of James, To those who have been called, who are loved by God the Father and kept by Jesus Christ: Mercy, peace and love be yours in abundance.

When we write formal letters in English to people or businesses we put the name of the recipient above the body of the letter on the left hand side of the page. Our own name and address will either go in the top right hand corner or across the top if we are using letter heading. Most languages have formal styles for letter writing, and this letter from Jude to a particular group of Christians kept to a recognised Jewish style. It gives the name of the one writing, the name or a description of those who are being addressed (verse 1), and then a greeting (verse 2).

However, although this book takes the form of a letter, it is very carefully crafted using traditional rhetorical devices, so that Jude, in effect, writes a sermon to his friends. As we work through the verses, we shall see just how skilled Jude was in his writing, and how he made his points hit home with great force.

The Greek of verse 1 says: '**Judas**, servant of Jesus Christ and brother of James.' Traditionally in English this Judas has been known as Jude presumably originally so no one would mistake him for the Judas who betrayed Jesus. However, there are a number of men in the New Testament called Judas, so it is important to identify, if we can, who the author of this letter actually is. Two serious contenders emerge. The first is Judas, the son of James, who was one of the twelve disciples and is mentioned in Luke 6:16 and Acts 1:13. He was also known as Thaddeus (see Matthew 10:3). The second is Judas, the brother of James and (half) brother of Jesus, who is mentioned in Matthew 13:55 and in Mark 6:3.

In the letters which the apostles Paul and Peter write they always state that they are apostles in their introduction. The only exceptions to this are where Paul is writing with Timothy or with Timothy and Silas who were not apostles (Philippians, 1 and 2 Thessalonians, and Philemon). If Jude had been an apostle we might have expected he would mention the fact. Not only does he not do so, but in verse 17 he seems deliberately to separate himself from the apostles. It thus seems that he cannot have been the apostle Judas, also known as Thaddeus. It does appear, then, that this Jude has to have been the Judas who is mentioned as the Lord's brother in Matthew 13:55 and Mark 6:3, where we find that another brother was called James. Jude says he is a 'brother of James'. The Lord's brothers were not members of the original twelve apostles though James, the Lord's brother, later took on an apostolic role in his position as leader of the church in Jerusalem (Acts 15:13; Galatians 1:19). He would thus have been well-known specially among Jewish Christian communities.

When did Jude, brother of Jesus, write this letter? We have very little information to go on, but can reasonably say that a brother of Jesus, even though he would have been younger, is unlikely to have written anything much after AD 85 simply because of age. The Palestinian Jewish flavour of the letter may suggest an earlier date. However, another factor seems to make a much earlier date possible. As noted in the Introduction to the commentary on 2 Peter, it is at least possible, if not likely, that 2 Peter was written *after* Jude. If this is the case, and Peter wrote 2 Peter (which we believe he did), then we have to date Jude sometime before the mid sixties when Peter was martyred in Rome for his faith. Beyond this, though, we can say little.

As we look at verse 1, then, we can account for Jude's mention of James and we can reasonably place him as the

Lord's brother. This also explains why Jude, correctly, does not use the label 'apostle'. But it remains a question as to why he did not refer to himself as the Lord's brother, but preferred to call himself **a servant of Jesus and a brother of James**.[3]

In a general sense, Jude was demonstrating his humility and lack of pretension. His description of himself says enough to establish his authority as a leader in the early church and yet does so in a gentle and humble way. In verse 3 he addresses his audience as **Dear friends**, thus identifying with them, as a leader, and yet as one who **shares** the same **salvation** as those to whom he speaks. It is this humble identification with other Christian friends that also comes through in his opening remarks.

In a more specific sense, though, we need to remember the word we translate as **servant** can be more accurately understood as 'slave' (*doulos* in Greek). Jude speaks out of an age in which slavery was well known. Many of the new Christians in the early church were slaves and slaves would have been seen walking the streets of any town in the Roman Empire of those days. Jude is therefore making a serious claim. Jesus had talked of how a person can be a 'slave to sin' (John 8:34), as did the apostle Paul in Romans 7:14. Christians have been redeemed from this slavery by the death

---

3. It is worth noting here that some commentators right through history have questioned whether Jude really wrote this epistle. One of the many arguments in favour of a belief that Jude, the Lord's brother, really did write this letter is that any pseudonymous author (one writing under the name of Jude and so claiming Jude's authority) would surely have appealed to being the brother of *Jesus*. A common reason given for not accepting the authorship as genuine was articulated clearly by Luther who said: 'This letter does not seem to have been written by the real apostle, for in it Jude refers to himself as a much later disciple of the apostles' (*Works*, Vol. 30, p. 203). Luther and others here have in mind verse 17. But there is no need to see verse 17 as indicating a much earlier period in church history (see comments on that verse).

of the Lord Jesus; they have now been 'set free' by Jesus (John 8:36). But Jude knows that the perfect freedom that is now his in Jesus involves accepting Jesus as *Lord and Master*. In one of the great paradoxes of the Christian life we discover that true freedom and enjoyment of life is found in total submission to the Lord, that is, in being **a slave of Jesus Christ**. As we shall see in verse 4, it was this that the false teachers had not grasped, but for Jude it underlies his whole life and teaching.

In an age when 'freedom' is once again a catch-word, when the cult of the 'self' insists on an individual's freedom to do whatever he or she wants, Christians must put forward service of Christ as the only ultimately satisfying life.[4] A beautiful old Anglican prayer puts it this way: '... in whose service is perfect freedom ...'[5]

So Jude, having humbly established his credentials as a leader, and having spelled out his position in life as one who is a slave of Jesus Christ, now tells us to whom he is writing. **To those who have been called, who are loved by God the Father and kept by Jesus Christ**. Jude does not mention where they live or even whether he had a hand in founding their church. Rather he is concerned to emphasise their position before God. These people to whom he is urgently writing are Christians because of the work of God himself. The consequence of this is that these people can know that whatever trouble comes from outsiders, they will remain **loved** by God the Father and they will continue to be **kept** by Jesus Christ.

---

4. It is important to understand that 'freedom' was very much a catchword of the secular philosophies of Jude's day. There is much to be said for the view that the false teachers Jude had to deal with were influenced in part by Epicurean philosophy. Epicureans affirmed that human sensations, preconceptions and feelings were the standard of truth; the end of all action was to be free from pain and fear.

5. From the Collect for Peace in Morning Prayer, from the Book of Common Prayer.

It is said by some that every good sermon has three points! Jude certainly uses repetition and groups of three words to impress truth upon his readers. Here is the first such group of words: **called, loved, kept**. Each individual word is important and full of wonderful biblical truth, but first we need to understand the general impact of what Jude is saying. If you read this sentence through again, you will see that it creates a general impression of *protected privilege*. While Jude no doubt wanted them to think of the implications of each separate word, it was the overall impact that was most important to him. These people were facing serious issues and, if they veered from the truth, they were in danger of being judged by God. They were going to be asked to **contend for the faith**, but they needed to know the base from which they could do that. Jude reminded them that their success in contending for the faith was in God's hands, for he had called them, loved them, and kept them. Jude's careful sermon-style letter begins with this point and ends with this point. In verses 24-25 he again reminds his readers that God will keep them, and the power to do so lies in God himself and in him alone. So much for the immensely important general point: *they are a wonderfully privileged people belonging to God who continues to keep them and protect them*. Let us now look at the individual words that Jude uses.

Called is a word often attached to God's people. It expresses the close relationship we have with God and reminds us of God's desire to save people from judgment. But it does much more than this. The background to this word is found in the Old Testament where we are reminded that in 'calling' his people to himself God took the initiative and brought Israel into being.

Sometimes in our church, when we have a special function, a 'call' goes out for people who will baby-sit so that parents with families can attend the meeting. The 'call' may be made

quite forcefully and for two or three Sundays in a row as part
of the regular notices but, at the end of the day, we cannot
compel people by calling for their help. In the Bible there is
a general call to all people to take responsibility for their sin
and turn to God. The gospel must be preached to all people,
but this is not the way the word 'call' is used here. The biblical
view of God's 'call' to his people is that it is *effective*. In this
sense God's call is what produces and **keeps** his covenant
people so that they can live holy lives that will be a witness
to other people and other nations. Isaiah 42:6 puts it this way:
'I, the LORD, have called you in righteousness; I will take
hold of your hand. I will keep you and will make you to be a
covenant for the people and a light for the Gentiles ...'

The apostle Paul also made it clear in Romans 8:30: 'And
those he predestined, he also called; those he called, he also
justified; those he justified, he also glorified.'

This is the sense in which Jude uses the word. For those
who belong to the Lord the word is full of encouragement
for it reminds them that God has taken the initiative because
he loved them, and it reminds them that he will keep them
and see them through to glory – which is just what Jude goes
on to say.

loved by God the Father again reminds us of the call of
God and the reason for his call. It is not that Christians
specially deserved God's love and favour. This is God's
unmerited favour to his people – his grace. For the people of
Israel, God's love was most clearly seen in the Exodus when
he redeemed his people from slavery in Egypt. In
Deuteronomy 7:6-8 God made this link between his call, his
love and the Exodus redemption very clear:

The LORD your God has chosen you ... to be his people, his
treasured possession. The LORD did not set his affection on you
and choose you because you were more numerous than other
peoples.... But it was because the LORD loved you... that he brought

you out with a mighty hand and redeemed you from the land of
slavery, from the power of Pharaoh king of Egypt...

In the New Testament, the people of God are identified
with those who have faith in Christ and they too are taught
that they are not called because they were special but because
God loved them. That love is most clearly seen in the final
and complete redemption achieved by Christ's death on the
cross. For New Testament writers, steeped in the teachings
of the Old Testament, what now happens in Christ is like a
'second exodus'. Those whom God calls are redeemed from
slavery to sin to freedom as the people of God. They are not
a 'new Israel', as some have chosen to describe the New
Testament people of God. That idea is alien to the Bible.
Rather those who have committed their lives to the gospel of
Christ *are* the people of God and so it must be expected that
what was addressed to the people of God in the Old Testament
is still addressed to them in the New. The difference between
Old Testament believers and those in the New Testament
lies in the fact that *in Christ* Christians have been privileged
to receive a much greater and deeper revelation of God than
was previously available.

Jude's statement here about God's love is perhaps better
translated as **loved *in* God the Father**. Jude's idea is one we
can all grasp and marvel at: God's call involves us being
caught up in and surrounded with his love. We are brought
into a community in which God actively works out his love
on our behalf.

Finally, Jude refers to his readers as those who are **kept**
by Jesus Christ. This again is a word which reminds us of
God's covenant love, his faithful and true love for his people.
We have already seen its Old Testament background in Isaiah
42:6. And the idea that God *keeps* his people for a purpose is
regularly taught in the Old Testament. In specifically saying
that these people are kept **by Jesus Christ**, we are reminded

of Jesus' words to his Father in the prayer before his death. Perhaps Jude also remembered what John recorded for us in John 17:12 – 'While I was with them, I protected them and kept them safe by that name you gave me.'

In the New Testament God's keeping of his people often has distinctly eschatological overtones.[6] In other words, it looks forward to the last days, the days of Christ's return, of judgment, and of eternal life. Jesus will keep his people right the way through life and even death until the time when he returns and they inherit full salvation in the presence of God himself.

This future perspective is vital for Jude and so he picks up on it again in verses 21 and 24. In verse 24 he refers to how God's people will be **kept** from falling so that eventually they will be presented before God in his glorious presence.

Surely there are few more wonderful teachings for us as Christians than this which we sometimes call the doctrine of *perseverance*. When we feel tossed this way and that, when we see the church torn by division, when we know that yet again we need God's forgiveness, when we reach a point of spiritual depression, then, above all, we should grasp with joy and wonder and thanksgiving the truth of Scripture that we are kept by Jesus Christ and that he will, in his mercy, bring us to eternal life (verse 21).

We have spent some time on this opening verse for it shows us much of Jude's view of the world and God's work among his people. It is a wholly uplifting verse and a verse that sets the context for Jude's warnings which follow. No matter how

---

6. 'Eschatological' is a word used to refer to 'talk about the last things', in other words, the day of judgment or the time when Christ returns, or inheriting the fulness of the kingdom of God etc. The New Testment as a whole has an 'eschatological perspective', that is, it has a perspective driven by the understanding that one day Christ will return, that there will be judgment, and Christians will one day fully inherit the eternal life of which the Spirit of God is the guarantee at present.

serious those warnings are, we know that we hear them in
the context of being a people called, loved and kept by God.

Mercy, peace and love be yours in abundance. Jude now
addresses his audience directly with a greeting similar in style
to many in Jewish writings. Some suggest that the greeting is
really asking that these people should themselves exhibit these
qualities of mercy, peace and love. Obviously Christians are
expected to do this as they imitate their Lord and Master. But
that is not really Jude's point here. Jude wants these Christians
to know and experience in their lives the covenant love and
mercy of God. Perhaps Jude uses the words in this order
because this is how Christians experience God's blessings in
their lives. First, they need God's mercy, which leads to peace
with God, and this in turn leads to a deeper experience of
God's love. However, really all three words are part of the
same prayer that Christians should know God's gracious work
in their lives.

In Jewish greetings the word translated as **mercy** denoted
God's steadfast covenant love. It described God's kindness
and faithfulness to his people. **Peace** was another 'covenant'
word which described the blessed (by God) state in which
people live if they have experienced such covenant love. The
Hebrew words lying behind the greeting are *hesed* (the
covenant love or mercy) and *shalom* (the covenant peace of
God experienced by those who have been forgiven and inherit
God's blessings). Verses like Isaiah 54:10 communicate well
the sort of blessings Jude, in his greeting, was praying the
church would see **in abundance** in their experience of life:

> "'Though the mountains be shaken and the hills be removed, yet
> my unfailing love for you will not be shaken nor my covenant of
> peace be removed," says the LORD, who has compassion on you.'

This verse in Isaiah reminds us that Jude's prayer is based on
the promises of God and therefore *is* being fulfilled and *will*

be fulfilled among the people whom he is greeting.

... and love be yours in abundance is a Christian addition to the Jewish greeting of 'mercy and peace'. Yet it is a natural way of drawing together the blessings God gives to his people. Jude makes God's covenant love an important theme in this letter. We have already seen it in verse 1 where we noted how Christians are 'loved in God the Father'. Now Jude draws together the greeting by praying that this love of God will 'be multiplied to you' (as the Greek puts it). Then in verse 21, Jude encourages people to **keep yourselves in the love of God**. Without God's enfolding faithful love there would be no hope for these Christians, for it is by God's love that his people are protected from themselves falling into sin and immorality.

Time and again complaints are heard from Christians about how evil society is today and how the church is really not much better. There is a despair in the voice of some Christians, but such is not a biblical attitude. It is proper to take sin and unchristian behaviour very seriously, specially when it affects church life as it was doing with Jude's people, but as we do that we must never underestimate God's covenant faithfulness. We need to maintain the perspective Paul articulated when praying for the Philippians; he was 'confident of this, that he who began a good work in you will carry it on to completion until the day of Christ Jesus' (Philippians 1:6).

2. Jude's reason for writing (verses 3-4)

Dear friends, although I was very eager to write to you about the salvation we share (verse 3).

Jude now begins the letter proper by explaining why he is writing. **Dear friends** is a translation of the Greek 'beloved' or 'loved ones'. Certainly it reflects Jude's own care for these

people, but it also continues Jude's theme that these people
are loved by God. For the third time in three verses, Jude
draws attention to God's love for them. They are **loved by
God** (verse 1), Jude prays they will know that **love in
abundance** (verse 2) and now addresses them as those who
are **beloved**. (See also Colossians 3:12 and 2 Thessalonians
2:13 where the apostle Paul makes similar points.)

**although I was very eager to write to you about the
salvation we share...** It is always good to draw attention to
things we have in common as Christians. Too often one
Christian can appear critical of another and too often
Christians can be too sensitive to well-intentioned advice from
another Christian that they take it as a personal insult. Indeed
it is perhaps one of the most destructive problems arising in
church life, that we are so often unable to listen to each other
because we are over sensitive to anything, however well-
intentioned, that may seem to border on criticism. Part of the
answer to this problem is that Christians must work at being
humble enough to hear what other brothers and sisters in
Christ are saying to them. Perhaps more important, though,
is that we all learn to draw attention first in any conversation
to those things that we have in common, those things in which
together we can rejoice and for which we can give thanks to
God. Jude does just this. He talks of the **salvation we share**.

Whatever events had overtaken him just before he began
to write this letter, Jude wanted them to know that he has not
just thought about writing to them because he has heard of
problems in their church. He had been going to write about
the greatest joy and privilege in life and this was held in
common between him and the Christians in this church.

How wonderful it would be if Christians were to see this
'common salvation' as the truth that should lie behind all
discussions, all challenges we may offer to each other, and
even all criticisms. Then, even the hardest of warnings and

criticisms will be seen to come in the context of the love of God for his people. Often Christians will rightly criticise the behaviour, the morality, or the doctrine of other Christians. That is their duty if they are concerned for each other's spiritual well-being, but this too often moves quickly into a condemnation of the other Christian which virtually suggests they are 'heretics' or that they were never really 'true' Christians after all. Jude's concern for this congregation emanates from his knowledge that the people share with him God's 'salvation'.

The wonder of salvation will be seen specially as Jude goes on to talk about a number of instances in history when God had judged evil-doers. In the church I attend, regular courses are run for those who are interested in becoming Christians or who have recently come to know Christ as Saviour and Lord. One question that is often asked of those taking the course is this: 'When we talk of salvation, what do you think we are saved from?' A number of answers come back. Just a few of the answers go like this: 'We are saved from our sin'; 'we are saved from the evil world around us'; 'we are saved from Satan'. All of these have some truth in them, but they do not get to the core of the word 'salvation'. What we share in common is that we are saved from *God*! It is *God's* judgment and *God's* justice that a person ought to fear if they do not know Christ. In verse 6, it was *God* who judged the angels and will judge them on the great Day. In verse 7 it was *God's* work to destroy Sodom and Gomorrah, and in verse 15 Jude makes it clear that the *Lord* will return to judge.

The wonder of salvation is that, in his mercy and love, God has saved his people from his own judgment which, in their sin, they deserve. This is what Christians and Jude and his readers have in common, and this is what we all **share**, forgiveness and the right not to face God's judgment on the last day. It was about this wonderful truth, this life-changing reality, that Jude had originally intended to write, but now he is forced to turn his pen to dealing with specific issues. Of course what he goes on to say is still in many ways concerned with **the salvation we share**, but it is focused on dealing with false teachers.

a) An urgent appeal (verse 3)

I felt I had to write and urge you to contend for the faith that was once for all entrusted to the saints.

For Jude there was a God-inspired need to write urgently asking the church to contend or fight for the faith. In 1 Corinthians 9:16 the apostle Paul uses the same word for the compulsion from God that he felt to preach the gospel, a compulsion that overtook all other considerations. So it is here with Jude. He feels compelled by God to write this letter. They must **contend for the faith**.

Contending implies that they must 'fight for' the faith. In the light of what is said later in the epistle about behaviour and works, they are no doubt expected to have to fight for the faith not just in the words they speak but also in their actions. The picture here is one of a military combat and it is perhaps an idea that does not sit too easily within our churches today. The Christian faith is about love and care and compassion. Gospel ministers are supposed to be nice and gentle, so the thought of some standing up and getting involved in what is best described as a 'fight' hardly goes down well. The problem with this modern approach is that it is undiscerning. It fails to take account of how serious some situations can be. In fact it is Jesus who once again can be our example. Think of how loving and compassionate and kind Jesus was to the untaught crowds who wanted to hear the truth and to see his miracles. Think of the grace he showed to the woman who came to him and washed his feet with her tears of repentance. Then think too of how he 'fought' in a completely uncompromising and forthright manner with the Pharisees who were not just destroying themselves with their hypocrisy but leading others astray as well. Look at Jesus speaking in Matthew 23:15: 'Woe to you, teachers of the law and Pharisees, you hypocrites! You travel over land and sea to win a single convert, and when he becomes one, you make him twice as much a son of hell as you are.'

Of course, we cannot see the heart of the person in front of us in the way Jesus could, but nevertheless we are expected to discern what is right and wrong according to the apostolic gospel and we must fight hard and clearly when people deliberately seek to undermine the truth. We shall see at the end of this letter of Jude that he too was well aware that some of the 'godless' people would be in a worse position than others. Some could be saved and some would continue to reject, but the church today, just as the church then, must realise that there are times when we must come out fighting. What Jude is saying here requires some pro-active work on the part of Christians and their leaders. But what is **the faith** for which they are to fight?

On the bookshelves of most ministers there are a number of books on 'theology'. Several by different writers are called 'Systematic Theology', and they look at a whole panoply of different doctrines in Scripture and show how the Christian biblical faith holds together and how different doctrines complement each other. Such books have enormous value. Some commentators have argued that it is this sort of thing that Jude is alluding to and, given that it would have taken many years to develop such a clear systematic framework of the doctrine of the whole Bible, this letter must have been written much later by someone other than Jude the brother of James.

There is no need at all to assume this. 'The faith' does not mean contending for some book summarising all of Christian doctrine or rushing to the defence of an early creed similar to those we say week by week in our Sunday worship. However, neither does 'the faith' refer to our own subjective belief and trust in Christ. Rather **the faith** is the truth which the apostles have preached about Jesus, and concerns **the salvation we share** with them.

The faith is unique

Elsewhere in the New Testament the same word is used to summarise the content of the Christian gospel that had been preached; so, for example, we read of the apostle Paul in Galatians 1:23 who is now 'preaching *the faith* he once tried to destroy'. In other places the same idea is caught up in the word 'gospel' (e.g. 1 Corinthians 1:17). There is a need to fight for this gospel truth which has led to their salvation. Without this unique truth there would be no salvation for Christians to share.

This faith is unchangeable

This faith, says Jude, **was once for all entrusted to the saints**. The saints here are those who are members of Christ's church. The word 'saints' means 'the holy ones', those referred to in verse 1 as 'called, and loved by God'. Of course, Jude has in mind specifically those to whom he is writing. They must continue to uphold and fight for the truth that they first heard and which first led them to Christ. This was 'once for all' delivered. In normal English usage we might say that they had received it 'once and for all'. It was not to be changed. Throughout the history of the church, heresy has entered as leaders and teachers have begun to think they know better than the simple basic 'once and for all' gospel of Jesus and his death on the cross for sinners.

Never has there been an age in which knowledge of our

world has expanded at such a speed. What an older generation took to be true in geography, physics and even mathematics, seems to be changing with every new discovery. It is not surprising therefore that people suggest that things should be added to the once and for all delivered faith. In a world where nothing lasts and it seems nothing is unchangeable, there is a temptation to assume the same is true of the Christian faith. Jude reminds his readers that the gospel message is unchangeable. The message of Christ dying for the sins of all who believe in him, the message of the resurrection, of conversion and forgiveness never changes.

This faith is apostolic

This faith was **entrusted**. The Greek word here might be translated as *handed down*. This does not imply a great length of time between the first time it was preached and the time Jude's readers heard of the faith. Rather the word brings to mind the handing down of teaching by word of mouth. It is a technical word from Jewish ways of teaching. The apostle Paul used it when relaying the instructions for the Lord's Supper in 1 Corinthians 11:2, 23. The word suggests a finished and complete body of teaching received by the people from their authoritative teachers. In the New Testament that teaching is therefore specifically linked with the apostles. What Jude is saying is that the message of the gospel which they had heard was the *apostolic* message. They may or may not have heard the message directly themselves from one or other of the apostles, but that is not the point. It was the apostle's teaching to which they had committed themselves, and that is the faith that is unique and unchanging. They and they alone were given by God the right to interpret the meaning of Jesus' death and resurrection, his teaching and his works.

Two thousand years later, we may express that message

in modern and relevant ways. We speak it in our own language rather than Greek, but we cannot and must not change the message, for it was handed down from the apostles and is unique and unchangeable. No wonder it is worth fighting for when people try to introduce new ideas or new teachings!

b) A very serious situation (verse 4)

For certain men whose condemnation was written about long ago have secretly slipped in among you. They are godless men, who change the grace of our God into a licence for immorality and deny Jesus Christ our only Sovereign and Lord.

Jude now expands upon the reasons for the urgent need to contend for the faith. **Certain** persons had **secretly slipped in among** them. Obviously this is only a minority of the congregation, but they will be able to cause untold harm if nothing is done about them. The very fact that they have gained entrance secretly makes it clear that there is a deliberate attempt to infiltrate and to change the church. As we saw in verse 3, whether they like it or not, the 'saints', the Christians in this church, have a fight on their hands. The question is whether they will realise it in time. This gives rise to the urgency of Jude's letter.

It is a sad fact that also in our generation there have been repeated attempts by different groups to 'worm their way into' churches. These false teachers are often not immediately recognisable. How nice it would be if they wore a placard round their necks saying 'I am a false-teacher'! But the truth is that they will often appear to be very friendly and kind, but their aim is to change the teaching of the church by adding to or taking away from the once and for all delivered faith. Time and again in recent years churches have been taken away from what was 'delivered'. Instead of focusing on the gospel of Christ crucified, people are encouraged to focus on self, on wealth and personal gratification, or even on health. Instead of focusing on imitating Christ in day to day life, people focus on being more like those around them in the world in which they live. The temptation for Christians to follow such bad teaching often lies in the fact that what is being taught has at least some basis in Scripture. So often Christians fail to realise that what may have started with Scriptural teaching has been grossly distorted and given a priority or a position way beyond that found in the Bible. The balance of the gospel is lost and people are led astray.

The temptation for any Christian, and indeed for the leaders and ministers in a church, is to try and live with such people because it is uncomfortable to stand up and 'contend'. If a leader really does 'contend' for the faith against such people who appear so nice and have so secretly been working for their goals, then the danger is that there will be a split in the congregation and, rightly, all Christians recoil from such an event. Nevertheless, if the church is to continue to be faithful to the gospel of Christ, then in some circumstances, the split will happen for that will be the outcome of serious battle for Jesus.

whose condemnation was written about long ago sounds rather surprising. Just who were these people and where were they written about? Before this can be properly answered, the rest of the verse must be examined for there we learn more of what these people were saying and doing.

They are godless men. If there is any word to sum up the general approach of these evil people it is this: they are **godless**. This is a theme that Jude repeats in his quotation from the book of Enoch in verse 15 (where forms of the word appear three times), and again in verse 18 where he sums up the situation by reference to the warnings of the apostles themselves. To be godless involves bringing shame upon God. It is, as we shall see, not a statement that they are atheists, but rather a description of their teaching and specially their *behaviour.* When the word is used in Jewish writings it is, as here, linked with the judgment that comes on the 'ungodly'.

The specific manifestation of their ungodliness is seen in two ways, says Jude. First, they are **immoral**. They **change the grace of our God into a licence for immorality**. The best way to describe these people is that they were *antinomian*. That is, they denied the need for, or application of, God's law.[7] We may find it hard to imagine how any Christian could deliberately propound immorality but, as was pointed out earlier, false teaching often has some basis in Scripture and this is what makes it apparently attractive. The apostles taught that Christ's death on the cross provided full forgiveness for his people. Christians' salvation is therefore not dependent upon themselves but upon God's gracious (undeserved and merciful) work in Christ. With the forgiveness of Christ they find the weight of guilt is gone and they are no longer condemned. The logic of the 'ungodly' might then proceed something like this: 'God forgives us by grace alone, and it doesn't matter what we do, we have not contributed to our salvation. Therefore it still doesn't matter what we do, because our salvation has nothing to do with our behaviour. Indeed, our ungodliness or immorality will only serve to show up God's grace all the more.' The apostle Paul anticipates a similar danger in teaching about grace in Romans 6:1: 'What shall we say, then? Shall we go on sinning, so that grace may increase?' Peter also spells out the danger of antinomianism in 1 Peter 2:16: 'Live as free men, but do not use your freedom as a cover-up for evil; live as servants of God.'

It is easy, therefore, to see how quickly one of the greatest teachings of all Scripture about God's love and mercy for his people can be distorted and taken out of context to produce a religion that is essentially 'ungodly'. In this context Jude's

---

7. From the Greek *anti*, meaning 'against', and *nomos* meaning law: 'against the law'.

second statement about the ungodly readily makes sense: they **deny Jesus Christ our only Sovereign and Lord**.

These people are living out a denial of the Lordship of Jesus in their lives. They are not so much teaching that Jesus is not Lord (if they had done that they would have been instantly recognisable by everyone as heretics), rather they are denying their Sovereign through their immoral behaviour. Luther put it like this: 'They regard themselves, not him, as their Lord.'

In Jude's introduction he called himself a 'slave' of Jesus Christ and slavery involves obedience and service. The faithful covenant God, to whom Jude called our attention in verse 1, calls his people to covenant obedience to the Master who has redeemed them and saved them. True disciples of Christ, those who *belong* to him through redemption, will desire to serve him and demonstrate their belief that he is their sovereign Lord. It is with these that Jude carefully identifies when he talks of Jesus as *our* only Sovereign.[8]

There are serious issues for all Christians in all ages to face up to in this verse. The Lordship of Christ over his people is a given in Scripture. It is the Christian's greatest joy and privilege to work for the Master. However, the Lordship of Christ is to be seen in every area of the Christian's life. There can be no 'Sunday only' Christians, as if Christ is not truly Lord when we go to work on Monday. There must be no 'no-go' areas in our lives of service to our Master and sovereign. If we refuse to let Jesus be Master in any area of our life as a Christian, then we are 'denying' him as sovereign. He cannot be Master of our home but not of our work. He cannot be Master of our marriages but not of our sex-lives. He cannot be Master of our heart but not of our business dealings. The Lordship of Christ must not just be a statement of faith but a

---

8. The word translated 'sovereign' means 'Master' and this more accurate term perhaps better implies the need for obedience among his servants.

truth that is lived out in every area of life. If this seems an impossible task, then we should remember that the mark of belonging to Christ and being adopted children and heirs of Christ is possession of the Holy Spirit. Thus we are not left alone to struggle to obey the Lord, but rather the Spirit enables us to live for Jesus day by day (see Romans 8:9-17).

Now we can return to the start of verse 4 and the words, **whose condemnation was written about long ago**. Where were these ungodly people spoken of previously and what is the condemnation of which Jude speaks? The words 'long ago' suggest Jude was not thinking of something he or even the apostles had said earlier. The fact that he now goes on to use examples from the Old Testament and from the book of Enoch suggests that he was looking back to much older prophecies and events. In the past there had been examples of the judgment that comes on the 'ungodly'. The early church was to take note of what was written beforehand and what had happened in the past. As the apostle Paul put it in 1 Corinthians 10:6 when he was dealing with a not too dissimilar situation in Corinth: 'Now these things occurred as examples to keep us from setting our hearts on evil things as they did.'

In recent years there has been a useful emphasis in the study of the Bible of looking first to see what the text meant in its original context. We are likely to miss something if we jump too quickly from the text to an immediate application to our day and age. However, at times it seems as if people have forgotten that the Old Testament is *throughout* useful in many varied ways for Christians. The apostle Paul in the verses just cited was referring to what the Corinthians should learn from the judgment that came upon the Israelites in the desert wanderings. This is just the example that Jude is about to move on to in verse 5.

As we look at ourselves or at the church at large today, we

need to ask ourselves whether the lesson has yet been learned. 'Godlessness' is judged by God, and those who apparently belong to him and seem to have received many of his blessings and benefits need to heed the warning most clearly. 'This condemnation', as Jude calls it here, has all been written about before. The verdict for such behaviour is already known, and it will be carried out on the last day at the return of Christ. The examples that are to follow in this letter served in God's plan as something of a 'foretaste' of the final dreadful judgment to be faced by all those who are godless in their behaviour and deny the Lord Jesus.

In this day and age there is too little emphasis on holiness of life and on 'godly' living as a mark of our service of Christ. Perhaps this has come from a serious effort not to re-introduce some sort of Pharisaical legalism as has happened at some periods of church history. But Jude knows, as do all the writers of Scripture, just how important holiness of life is as an appropriate response to the Lordship of the one and only sovereign. Just as 'ungodly' is a repeated refrain in this letter, so is the opposite. Christians are 'saints', the 'holy ones' (verse 3), the angels who are coming with the Lord are 'the holy ones' (verse 14), the congregation must build itself up in its most 'holy' faith (verse 20), and finally those who do serve the Lord will be presented 'without fault' ('unstained', verse 24) before God on that final judgment day. Jude could not be clearer. The one group are heading for eternal life and the other for condemnation, and the latter will have no excuse, for they knew all about it!

3. Good grounds for urgency (verses 5-7)

Though you already know all this, I want to remind you that the Lord delivered his people out of Egypt, but later destroyed those who did not believe (verse 5).

 The sense of urgency that Jude has conveyed about the dangers these Christians are facing is now pressed home with three vivid illustrations of the way in which those who have apparently seemed secure and who have even seemed to be 'holy' have ended up being judged. The first illustration calls upon the church to recall the most famous of all such incidents, namely the destruction of many 'godless' Israelites even after they had actually been brought out of slavery in Egypt by God.

a) Remember what happened to the Israelites (verse 5)

This example is the natural one with which to begin. It had been used again and again throughout the history of God's people. The Israelites, who had been slaves for so many years under the Pharaohs of Egypt, had been redeemed from that slavery by God himself and had been led towards the promised land by Moses, God's servant. The Exodus was looked back upon as the ultimate demonstration of God's love and redeeming power for his people. As mentioned earlier, so important was that event that some of the New Testament writers regarded the redemption from slavery to sin by the death and resurrection of Christ as a sort of 'second exodus' – the final and greatest redemption. The power of the illustration, though, lies in the warning it carries. Many Israelites had experienced the exodus from Egypt and had clearly seen the power of God, yet they had begun to take the grace and mercy of God for granted. The book of Numbers vividly describes how time and again the people complained about their conditions but, more than that, they eventually denied God's Lordship by their actions and turned to sexual sin and idolatry. It is to this that Jude now refers.

Though you already know all this, I want to remind you ... This illustration of the way the Israelites were blessed by God but then perverted his grace and acted immorally

was one of which this Christian congregation would already
have been well aware. All Christians quickly became
acquainted with the Old Testament, but this congregation with
a Palestinian background would have been specially aware
of these examples from history. This was part of the 'faith
that was once for all entrusted to the saints' (verse 3). Unlike
the false leaders, Jude was not now adding to the basic gospel,
but simply drawing attention to how they should apply that
faith to this situation.

In this day and age, even in parts of the church, many
deny the historical reliability of whole sections of the Bible.
But it was part and parcel of Jewish belief, and is essential to
true Christian faith, that God is a God of history whose actions
have been recorded in holy Scripture as a true record of his
dealings with men and women through the ages. In looking
carefully at the way God has spoken to men and women and
acted for them and even against them in judgment, future
generations of God's people learn about God. As Paul says
to Timothy in 2 Timothy 3:16, this means that Christians
should regard *all* Scripture as profitable. In the case of the
examples Jude now gives, they are specially profitable by
way of *warning* and *correction*.

**that the Lord delivered his people out of Egypt, but
later destroyed those who did not believe.**[9] Many
commentators plausibly suggest that the specific event in
Israelite history to which Jude referred concerned the disbelief
of the people when the spies returned to their camp in the
desert from spying out the Promised Land. Ten spies were
very fearful of the people already in Canaan, while Joshua
and Caleb argued that, with God on their side, the conquest
of the Promised Land would be possible. In Numbers 14:11

---

9. The word 'later' translates the Greek 'second time' (*to deuteron*). The
idea of the verse may be reasonably interpreted like this: 'the Lord who was
(first) enountered delivering his people out of Egypt was next (secondly)
seen to destroy those who did not believe.'

we read of God's judgment on that generation. 'The LORD said to Moses, "How long will these people treat me with contempt? How long will they refuse to believe in me, in spite of all the miraculous signs I have performed among them?' Belief and trust in God was the issue here. And that fits well with Jude's reference to the destruction of those **who did not believe**.

Though the issue in Numbers 14 was disbelief, and Jude draws attention to this, that incident did not involve sexual immorality or licentiousness, nor did it *specifically* deny the covenant Lordship of God[10] which are both Jude's concern here. In the next two examples immorality and Lordship are issues and in the explanation of the examples in verse 8 Jude says: **In the very same way, these dreamers pollute their own bodies, reject authority...** It is therefore worth asking whether Jude might have had some other incident in mind where the Israelites were condemned not just for their lack of faith but also for their immorality and denial in practice of God's covenant Lordship.

A real possibility here is the passage that is referred to in a number of other contexts in Scripture which also seek to draw lessons from the Israelites' wanderings in the desert. In Numbers 25 we read about Israelite men who 'began to indulge in sexual immorality with Moabite women, who invited them to the sacrifices of their gods ... So Israel joined in worshipping the Baal of Peor. And the Lord's anger burned against them' (verses 1-3). Worship of other gods and sexual immorality often went hand in hand in Israelite history, and this would undoubtedly fit well with what Jude is seeking to illustrate. The practice of sexual immorality in a context of the worship of other gods clearly highlights Jude's concern over immorality but also its direct relationship to a denial of

---

10. Of course, any disobedience of God is a denial of his Lordship in one sense, but this was not the intention of the Israelites in Numbers 14 who were, after all, scared and lacking in faith.

the covenant 'Master' and Lord. It is also important to note that this incident from Numbers is repeated through Israel's history by way of warning against both idolatry (a denial of the only Lord) and sexual immorality.

When Moses looks back at the time in the wilderness and draws lessons from their experiences he refers to this incident and says, 'Do not add to what I command you and do not subtract from it, but keep the commands of the LORD your God that I give you. You saw with your own eyes what the LORD did at Baal Peor. The LORD your God destroyed from among you everyone who followed the Baal of Peor, but all of you who held fast to the LORD your God are still alive today' (Deuteronomy 4:2-3). Notice here how Moses applies the lesson: no one is to add to or subtract from what was delivered to them by the Lord through Moses. It reminds us, surely, of Jude's argument that we have a 'once and for all delivered faith'. The next occasion when the Israelites are asked to remember the incident of Baal Peor is in Joshua 22:16-17. Here the Israelites speak to members of the tribes of Reuben, Gad and Manasseh and specifically draw out the issue of *faith*: 'The whole assembly of the LORD says: "How could you break faith with the God of Israel like this? How could you turn away from the LORD and build yourselves an altar in rebellion against him now? Was not the sin of Peor enough for us?" ' Later the Psalmist also takes up the same lessons from the years of desert wanderings. Psalm 78 shows very clearly how future generations of Israelites were to learn from God's dealings with them and specially previous judgments and blessings. Again in Psalm 106 the message comes through and Baal Peor is one of several examples (verses 28-31). Even prophets like Hosea (9:10) beg Israel to return to the Lord rather than suffer the way of the Israelites at Baal Peor.

In the New Testament, too, the same warning taken from

Baal Peor is given by Paul to the Corinthians who were indulging in some form of sexual immorality (1 Corinthians 10:6-8). Drawing on Numbers 14, the writer to the Hebrews (chapters 3-4) also warns that we should learn from the past.

It is worth spending time in each of these passages of Scripture before coming back to Jude, to see just how important it is to learn from history even for us today. There are good grounds for urgency. Judgment awaits those who do not believe and who take advantage of the grace of God. We cannot get away from the fact that we as Christians are in direct line of continuity with the covenant people of God in the Old Testament. The new covenant reaches out to all nations, not just Israel, and it reveals much that was not there for the Israelites to see, but the dangers for us are the same as they have always been for any member of God's covenant family. We must not become arrogant and proud for, as Paul puts it in 1 Corinthians 10:12, just when we think we stand before God we may find we fall. Immoral and licentious behaviour makes a mockery of God's grace and love and will lead to his judgment just as certainly as it did for those at Baal Peor. Adding to or subtracting from **the faith that was once for all entrusted to the saints** is serious indeed and no less so for us today than for those in the early church or those who sat under the leadership of Moses.

b) Remember what happened to fallen angels (verse 6)

The second example of judgement that Jude draws on was probably specially appropriate for his particular audience and may sound a little strange to our ears. Jude's audience would have been well read in Hebrew Scriptures, of course, but they would also have been acquainted with the religious literature that was popular in their day, even if it was not part of the canon of Scripture. The example which follows is based firmly in Scripture and yet in its structure, style and detail seems to show dependence upon a book we know as the Book of Enoch which was written during intertestamental times, probably completed by about 200 BC. An appendix on Jude's use of Enoch is found on pages 231-234 and should be read in connection with this verse, but is also specially relevant to verses 9 and 14-15.

And the angels who did not keep their positions of authority but abandoned their own home – these he has kept in darkness, bound with everlasting chains for judgment on the great Day.

Here Jude draws on 1 Enoch 6-19 in which 'Enoch' gives an account of how angels fell from glory through rebellion and sin. The story is based around an elaboration of a rather enigmatic text in Genesis 6:1-4. In the biblical text this is a lead-in to the account of the judgment of the flood. It talks of how the numbers of people on earth were growing rapidly and how their sin continued (verse 1). Part of God's judgment was to be a limitation on the length of their lives to 120 years (verse 3). Most of this is straight-forward enough, but we also read: 'the sons of God saw that the daughters of men were beautiful, and they married any of them they chose' (verse 2), and (verse 4): 'The Nephilim were on the earth in those days – and also afterward – when the sons of God went to the daughters of men and had children by them. They were the heroes of old, men of renown.'

As mentioned in the Appendix, intertestamental teachings specially emphasised angelic activity. In Enoch these verses from Genesis 6 are taken to refer to angels ('the sons of God') who sinfully lusted after human women and had sex with them, resulting in the birth of the giants of old. These angels were then subject to the judgment of God who did not destroy them but has kept them 'in chains' under the earth for the final judgment day when they will be banished to eternal fire. Enoch's account elaborates on this in all sorts of far-

fetched detail, giving names to the leaders of the angels and
suggesting that the angels helped teach human beings about
even greater depths of sin.

Whether Genesis 6 is talking about angels at all has long
been a matter of debate. Very early Christian writers
understood it in the way these intertestamental Jewish texts
did but, later, as people studied the passage more closely the
majority, as today, realised that 'sons of God' was more likely
a reference to the men who were in the world at the time. But
this is not Jude's concern here.[11]

**these he has kept in darkness, bound with everlasting
chains for judgment on the great Day**. The point Jude is
making is this: Once these angels, who of all beings had
known the joy and blessings of existence with God, had
rebelled, they were set on a course for the final judgment
which was inevitable and inescapable. The idea of being **kept
in darkness** when it would seem they still have the freedom

---

11. There are, of course, other passages of Scripture that people believe
offer further glimpses of Satan's fall from glory, his rebellion against God,
and the way other angels followed him. See, for example, Isaiah 14:12-13
and Ezekiel 28:11-19. The fact of the matter is that, apart from serving as an
example from which we must learn, what happened to angels and God's
subsequent judgment of them is really not the business of human beings!
Speculation on such matters is once again leading the church away from the
substance of the gospel into myths and fantasies. This is a feature of much
'New Age' teaching and it has infiltrated its way back into the church with
all sorts of fantastical claims about angels and their work among us. Jude
lived in a day when such myths abounded. We could do well to learn from
him, that he limits his use of such stories to making a point that is valid for
all time: rebellion against God and sexual immorality leads to judgment as
much for us as for angels.

If the 'sons of God' in Genesis 6 are male humans beings, then it is not
clear why they rather than the women should be linked to God. Perhaps it is
because the men, who were descended from faithful ancestors like Enoch,
were held responsible for leading the people into sexual immorality.

Note: much of this footnote section is repeated in the commentary on 2
Peter in order to avoid unnecessary cross-referencing for those who are
only studying this epistle.

to act in the present age, confirms the view that the issue is the certainty and inevitability of their final judgment. Just as Christians are **kept by Jesus Christ** (verse 1) as they **keep themselves in God's love** waiting for that final day that will bring their salvation (verse 21), so these angels are being kept by the same Lord for the same final day. The difference is that they are being **kept** for condemnation on that day.

Jude's logic is clear and his urgency dynamic: *if the certainty of final judgment is true for angels who have rejected God's Lordship and have become immoral, how horrifically true it will also be for those who teach such things in the church of Christ.*

Jude has reminded his readers of the problem the Israelites faced, and of judgment upon the angels. Both examples would have been well known to the Christians to whom Jude was writing. The third and final example at this point, though, is one that is even known in our day and age by people who are not Christians! From our point of view it is probably the most obvious biblical example of sexual immorality and a denial of the Lordship of God.

c) Remember what happened to Sodom and Gomorrah (verse 7)

In a similar way, Sodom and Gomorrah and the surrounding towns gave themselves up to sexual immorality and perversion. They serve as an example of those who suffer the punishment of eternal fire.

All three examples Jude has used are designed to call forth a response of outrage from the readers. According to an intertestamental Jewish book known as the Book of Wisdom (10:7), the region of Sodom and Gomorrah was apparently still smoking even in Jude's days. The Book of Enoch, to which we have just been referring, describes the place where the angels have been imprisoned (1 Enoch 67:4-13) as a place which is smoking.

But of course, the Biblical writers themselves had referred on many occasions to God's judgment on those cities with a view to eliciting repentance from people in their own generation. Isaiah, Jeremiah, Hosea, Amos and Zephaniah are all prophets in the Old Testament who make mention of the sin of these cities and the judgment that came upon them. Jesus himself compares the Pharisees with the inhabitants of those towns.

In a similar way, Sodom and Gomorrah and the surrounding towns gave themselves up to sexual immorality and perversion. The sin of Sodom and Gomorrah and its subsequent judgment is of course another example in which sexual immorality and a denial of the covenant Lord is seen. The happenings on that fearful day are recounted in Genesis 19:1-11. The Lord had spoken to Abraham in chapter 18 through his angels and had warned Abraham about the coming judgment on Sodom. Abraham was very disturbed because that was where his nephew Lot was living. He interceded for the cities. In chapter 19 we read how two angels then arrived in Sodom where they met Lot who greeted them and invited them home. After they had eaten and 'before they had gone to bed', the house was surrounded by the men of the city insisting that these 'men' be brought out 'so that we can have sex with them' (verse 5). Lot refused, and even offered the men his daughters instead, but the crowd refused to listen. They even threatened Lot himself. In the end the angels took matters into their own hands and struck blind the men outside. They then gathered Lot and his family together and quickly left the city. In God's providence the incident, of course, made it abundantly clear to Lot that he should not be living in such a town and it also served to show just how righteous was the subsequent judgment of God upon the city.

The sin of the city was enormous. This particular incident makes it clear the people there were prepared to become involved in homosexual gang rape; that they could do this to strangers, indicated their disdain for other people and lack of hospitality so traditional to those societies. When the prophet Ezekiel warned the people of Jerusalem of their sin (Ezek. 16:49-50), he referred back to the sin and judgment of Sodom like this: 'Now this was the sin of your sister Sodom: She and her daughters were arrogant, overfed and unconcerned; they did not help the poor and needy. They were haughty and did detestable things before me. Therefore I did away with them as you have seen.' It is interesting that their sin was more than the 'detestable practices' that no doubt included gang rape and other sexual perversions, for it also included a general arrogance and disdain for the Lordship of God in all areas of life.

As Jude picks it up by way of example, he is concerned, of course, about learning from the judgment upon the city. As in the previous examples he no doubt chose this one because of the issue of Lordship and sexual immorality. The angels came from the Lord as his mouthpiece and even Lot had been unable to protect them. The attack on the angels was a clear example of the men's refusal to listen to anyone but themselves, hence Ezekiel's reference to their arrogance. But the practice of homosexual rape was also an indication of the level of sexual perversion in a society where homosexuality was apparently regarded as preferable to heterosexual activity. The daughters were, after all, turned down (although surely Lot was sinful in even thinking of offering his daughters to such men).

In verse 7 in the Greek Jude says this: *Just as Sodom and Gomorrah and the surrounding cities which took part in sexual immorality and followed after strange flesh serve as an example* ... From Jude's point of view probably two sexual issues are in mind and both indicated the heinous nature of such immorality. First, 'strange flesh' may well be a reference in Jude's thinking to the fact that these men of Sodom were trying to have sex with angels, the opposite way round to the angels who were judged for wanting sex with human women! But 'strange flesh' probably also has in mind the homosexual activity. After all, Genesis 19 gives us no indication at all that the men of Sodom had any knowledge that these 'foreigners' were anything other than normal *men*.

They serve as an example of those who suffer the punishment of eternal fire. The area where Sodom and Gomorrah had once existed at the south end of the Dead Sea was still, even in Jude's day, an area of smoking sulphur. These cities, therefore, 'are shown as an example'. The judgment on Sodom and Gomorah was so devastating and horrific, and still visible so many centuries later, that the two cities became a bye-word for judgment, even as they are today.

So in verses 5-7 Jude has listed three obvious examples of God's judgment on people who had rejected the Lord God's authority and had indulged in various forms of sexual depravity. The fact that all three groups had indulged in sexual immorality of a different sort suggests that Jude was not actually singling out particular sexual activity as specially worthy of judgment so much as sexual immorality generally. It is unlikely that the false leaders in the congregation to which Jude was writing were involved in homosexual activity or in suggesting sexual activity with the angels. Once again, if this had been the case they would have been easily identified as heretics and would not easily have 'secretly slipped in among' them. Nevertheless, Jude demonstrates by these examples that a variety of sexual immorality to be found in Scripture all ended in fearful judgment, and that such activity was directly linked to a denial of the covenant Lord.

Special Lessons for Today

As we seek to apply these verses to the modern church, we must be aware of just how easy it is to slip into sexual immorality if we move away from obedience to the demands of Jesus our Lord and Saviour. It is easy to think it would never happen to us! But let's pause here a moment and look at the first and last example again. Notice how *groups* of people are affected. Some were no doubt led on by others. As a form of behaviour is found acceptable by some and then perhaps justified, so others get drawn in. Whichever incident Jude had in mind, the happenings at Baal Peor (Numbers 25) or the incident with the Golden Calf (Exodus 32), both reveal just how quickly the whole community came to accept something that only a few months before, let alone years, would have been regarded as unforgivable. The problem at Sodom and Gomorrah was truly awful, but here was a whole community for whom such behaviour had apparently become acceptable to the extent that Lot's voice was as a 'stranger' and 'foreigner' even though he had lived there for years. We must never underestimate two pressures which come on us as Christians. The first is that we are tempted to excuse and eventually accept that which the world around us accepts in terms of sexual behaviour, and the second is that we begin to accept uncritically what some Christians do and gradually bow to peer pressure to the extent that we begin to justify actions that would have been unacceptable only a few years before.

We may wish to distinguish between some very serious and dreadful sexual depravity like homosexual gang rape and committing adultery, but both are sexual immorality and both involve a denial of Christ's Lordship in our lives if we go that route. Often we hear people applying Jude's teaching specially against the sin of homosexuality, and surely it is right to apply the text in that direction. However, it is also

right to see that young people having sex with a partner before
getting married is immoral behaviour before God. Some
Church of England ministers now find that about 90% of the
couples coming to them to get married have already been
living together for some time. While they would no doubt
want to affirm these couples in their desire to get married, it
is far more difficult to speak against a sin that is so widely
accepted by society. After all, the minister might then be
upsetting Mrs. 'so-and-so' whose daughter is living with a
boyfriend and who is 'such a lovely Christian'. Indeed the
minister may have a son who is doing the same and, 'after
all, the issue is being faithful to one partner rather than actually
being *married*, isn't it?'

Anyone who is involved in the real issues of the world
and church life today will identify immediately with these
sorts of pressures to conform to less than God's will exerted
not just by pagan society around but even by Christians. Or
take as another example the way Christians so often fail to
condemn adultery. Some years ago a couple who called
themselves Christians asked if they could get re-married and
have their wedding 'blessed' in a church service. (Our
denomination does not at present allow the re-marriage in
church of divorcees.) I talked to them about the matter, only
to discover that neither was yet divorced and that both were
currently still married to partners who were also Christians!
But neither could 'get on' with their current husband/wife
and 'God had called them' to divorce and marry each other.
As you may imagine the discussion went on for some time at
a variety of levels. 'How can God call you to do something
he expressly prohibits in his word?' 'Is it really impossible
to work at making your current marriages successful to God's
glory?' And so the conversation progressed. No amount of
talk or reference to Scripture seemed to make any difference
to them and eventually I had to refuse them. The interesting

thing was that the couple seemed to understand that position even if they disagreed with it. A number in the congregation asked how I could possibly be so harsh and mean as obviously these two were 'trapped' in unacceptable marriages and we ought to 'affirm them as people'. How subtle is the way in which Christians move towards acceptance of a position that is sinful in the eyes of God.

People will argue that what is going on may be 'less than God's will' but it's not as bad as it might be. We need to remember, though, that 'less than God's will' is also 'sin' and hence a denial in practice of his Lordship in that area of our lives.

The issue of homosexual practice has also reared its head in serious debates in many Christian denominations. For most Christians and indeed many non-Christians, this practice is regarded as so obnoxious that there is a temptation in some circles to be more quick to denounce this sin than to denounce other sexual sins such as those we've just mentioned. However, again in some churches there are leaders who are subtly seeking to undermine the view that this is a sin. 'Gang rape' they say is a sin. Infidelity to one's partner is a sin, but God is not against a loving, kind, and faithful sexual relationship between a couple just because they are from the same sex. This is of course a sort of moral blackmail. If we say God is against it, we are apparently being asked to make God into some kind of monster who doesn't care for these lovely kind and faithful people. Though this is not the place to debate the understanding of each biblical text that tackles this issue, we must remember that the way we tackle the issue must always seek to bring together the covenant Lordship of Christ with the issue of sin. As we have seen, Jude holds these two together. God asks us all to make what often seem to be difficult sacrifices. For some those sacrifices will have to do with temptations to sexual sin and the need to live a

pure and holy life for him. For others those sacrifices will
have to do with choices about materialism or doing what God
has called them to. But, as Christians, we must realise that to
go against God's will is to **deny Jesus Christ our only
sovereign and Lord**.

Standing up against the pressures of society and even
arguing with Christian teachers like those of Jude's day who
seem so persuasive in their logic and so compassionate in
their concern for individuals will not be easy for any of us.
To stand up against them with the love of Christ, with real
concern for them as individual human beings, will be even
harder. Jude returns to that point in verse 22.

4. These godless people also face judgment (verses 8-13)

We now come to the fourth section of this epistle in which
Jude applies these examples to the 'certain men' who have
secretly entered the church.

**In the very same way, these dreamers pollute their own bodies,
reject authority and slander celestial beings** (verse 8).

They are **dreamers** in the sense that they are like 'false
prophets'. That is, false teachers and prophets used to claim
that they had been given their teachings or their authority
from God through a dream. Perhaps one of the clearest
examples of God's damning criticism of those who claim
such authority is found in Jeremiah 23:25-32. There the
prophet Jeremiah proclaimed God's judgment on such people
with the words of the Lord:

'I have heard what the prophets say who prophesy lies in my name.
They say, "I had a dream! I had a dream!" How long will this continue
in the hearts of these lying prophets, who prophesy the delusions of
their own minds? They think the dreams they tell one another will make
my people forget my name, just as their fathers forgot my name through
Baal worship.... "Is not my word like fire," declares the LORD, "and like
a hammer that breaks a rock in pieces? Therefore," declares the LORD, "I

am against the prophets who steal from one another words supposedly from me.... Indeed, I am against those who prophesy false dreams," declares the LORD. "They tell them and lead my people astray with their reckless lies, yet I did not send or appoint them. They do not benefit these people in the least," declares the LORD.'

Jude's passing comment here reminds us that these false leaders were not just practising immorality but actually teaching and encouraging it, even claiming a received authority for what they did and said.

Jude's point here is simple. In the same way as those of history were polluted by sexual sin, so these people have polluted their own bodies by sexual sin, giving it an aura of having come as a message from God. Sexual pollution of bodies we have seen in each of the three examples, but Jude moves on. They **reject authority**... Again each example has shown clearly how such sexual sin has denied the only Lord and Master, rejecting the authority of the covenant Lord. ... **and slander celestial beings**. This is a little less clear in all three examples. In the last example of Sodom and Gomorrah Jude is, no doubt, referring to the fact that these men were prepared to rape angelic beings (even if they did not know that is who they were). The middle example of the angels fits well with Jude's point, as angels themselves refused to keep the position given them by God. But the first example of the wilderness generation does not immediately seem to relate to celestial beings. Of course, there is no special reason why Jude should make each example fit his application in every single point except that Jude is so carefully structured that we might expect a reference even in this example to angels being slandered.

The most likely explanation here is one that will not immediately be apparent to us but was probably seen quite quickly by his readers. In Acts 7:38 and 53, Stephen, the martyr, accused his assailants of not obeying the law of Moses which was given and put into effect by angels. The same

point is made in Hebrews 2:2. In Galatians 3:19 the apostle
Paul also talked of the role the angels had in putting the law
into effect. In early Jewish writings more was said of this
role, but it is clear from the Biblical evidence that the angels
were entrusted with upholding in the world the moral order
that was described in the law of Moses. Thus Jude's first
example also fits with his saying that these false teachers
'slander celestial beings'. He is simply saying that those who
brought the word of God's message and law are being
slandered as that message and law are deliberately broken.
Jude has said they **deny Jesus Christ our only Sovereign
and Lord**. Now, in a different way, he points out the same
truth – they have slandered the ones who are the messengers
of the Sovereign Lord by their refusal to listen to or obey the
message.

Special Lessons for Today

It is sadly all too common today to hear people talk of having
had a dream in which God has told them to do something or
in which he has revealed to them something about the future
or even about the end of the world. Such 'dreams' used to be
seen quickly for the lies they were. Even untrained Christians
were healthily sceptical and asked whether the dream could
be tested against 'the faith that was once for all entrusted to
the saints'. In other words, people who made such claims
had their teachings tested against Scripture. Most were seen
quickly to be heretical and dangerous. Perhaps earlier
generations took Jude more seriously!

Nowadays we live in a world where dreams are regularly
being 'interpreted' by church members. It is interesting that
this is also very much a part of the world in which we live.
We find dreams and their interpretations featuring
prominently in the New Age movement. We also find a
tendency in our world, where 'Postmodernism' is so much

in vogue, and where the 'assured' results of reason and science are now so questioned, to look to other ways than reason and scientific endeavour for coming to 'knowledge'. Here too dreams figure in many writings. In other words, without going into great detail about the philosophies of the world that surround Christians today, we certainly once again live in a period where people are beginning to justify life actions and 'religious' beliefs on the basis of dreams and other subjective experiences.

While reason and the scientific endeavour are also often thoroughly inimicable to the Christian faith, we must realise that we now face other attacks and dangers. To us they may be 'new'. When we look back at Jude, we have to say that 'there is nothing new under the sun', and God's word of the past stands as a warning to us today. Just as Jude used Old Testament examples for his day and age, so we are called upon to look at *both* Old Testament warnings of God's judgment *and* at Jude's New Testament warnings to his generation. When we hear of people trying to justify a particular course of action on the basis of a vision or a so-called revelation or a dream, let us return, as Jude asks us to, to God's Word in Scripture and test what we see and hear.

It is perhaps one of the saddest aspects of church life today that we often come across Christians who would much rather believe a 'dream' or 'vision' from a Christian friend than they would spend time immersed in learning for today from the Word of God in the way Jude demonstrates to us. This is a reflection in the church of many aspects of the thinking of the world around us. When Christians are seen to spend much time discussing someone's dream or vision, it surely has to be said that, whatever its value may or may not be, the real commitment of time should be to Scripture and testing all our words and behaviour against the one place where we know for certain we have God's mind on matters.

> But even the archangel Michael, when he was disputing with
> the devil about the body of Moses, did not dare to bring a
> slanderous accusation against him, but said, 'The Lord rebuke
> you!' Yet these men speak abusively against whatever they do
> not understand; and what things they do understand by
> instinct, like unreasoning animals – these are the very things
> that destroy them (verses 9- 10).

Jude now asks his readers to consider three points of comparison so he can make the application to 'these men' even clearer.

a) Compare their behaviour with the archangel Michael's behaviour (verse 8-10)

The story to which Jude now refers comes from a Jewish elaboration upon the Biblical passages which speak of the death and burial of Moses and of the archangel Michael, who defends God's people in both the Old Testament and New. Below we try to piece together the background for this example that Jude uses. However, the application is clear even from the short comments Jude gives us.

... even the archangel Michael, when he was disputing with the devil about the body of Moses ... Jude refers to an argument between the archangel Michael, and the devil over the burial of the body of Moses. Even with all his power and even as the protector of God's people with right on his side, the archangel Michael would not take the law into his own hands as 'these men' were doing – ignoring bits they didn't like and no doubt playing on that which suited them.

... did not dare to bring a slanderous accusation against him, but said, 'The Lord rebuke you!' Even Michael, having won the battle with Satan, left that being in the hands of the Lord God to pronounce judgment rather than himself judge a celestial being. Using words from Zechariah 3:1-2, Michael said 'The LORD rebuke you.' While the background is both perplexing and interesting, we must not forget as we go more deeply into it that the application is straight-forward enough – compare these men and their behaviour with the archangel Michael's behaviour!

Excursus[12]: Michael, an accusation and the dispute over the body of Moses

The death and burial of Moses are mentioned in the Old Testament, but there is no mention of any dispute between Michael and the Devil about the matter. In Deuteronomy 34:6 we are told that God buried the body of Moses in Moab near Beth Peor and that no one knows where the body was buried.

Michael, whose name means 'Who is like God?', is mentioned in the Book of Daniel and of Revelation. In Daniel 10:13, 21 there is a reference to 'Michael, one of the chief princes' who was involved in helping the people of Israel during the time of the Babylonian captivity. Later, in chapter 12:1, Michael is mentioned as the one who will arise in the last days. He is 'the great prince who protects [the] people [of God]'. In 1 Thessalonians 4:16, talk of an 'archangel' who will appear with Christ at the end of time is almost certainly another reference to Michael. In Revelation 12:7, 'Michael and his angels fought against the dragon' and won so that the dragon (Satan) lost his place in heaven together with his own angels who followed him.

The reference to Zechariah 3:2 ('The Lord rebuke you!' in Jude 9) is set in the context of a vision of a courtroom scene. Here a high priest called Joshua stands before 'an angel of the LORD' (verse 1), and Satan stands beside Joshua to accuse him. In the courtroom drama we have a wonderful example of one who, though a high

---

12. Much of this excursus is repeated in the commentary on 2 Peter in order to avoid unnecessary cross-referencing for those who are only studying this epistle.

priest, is a sinner. As Satan fulfils his role of seeking to accuse God's people of sin, so the angel steps forward to say that Joshua's sin has been removed. In verse 2 in the Hebrew it is the Lord himself who says 'The Lord rebuke you, Satan!' Jude probably had a version in which it continued to be the angel of the Lord who was speaking as in much of the rest of the chapter.

This is the extent of the Biblical information. Our problem, therefore, in understanding all this is that nowhere in the Bible except here in Jude do all these references come together nor are they made to fit in with each other. However, in a number of intertestamental Jewish writings Satan is regarded as the accuser who tries to undo or challenge the work of God's people and of 'the angel of the Lord'. The problem of understanding these two verses in Jude was nearly as acute for the very early New Testament commentators as it is for us. But they had before them another piece of Jewish writing known as the *Testament of Moses*. We only have a late Latin version of this document, but Clement of Alexandria, Origen and other early Christian teachers and writers seem to have had a complete and longer writing, probably in Hebrew or Aramaic, from which they believed Jude drew the story he used here.

Richard Bauckham in his commentary[13] on this epistle has sought carefully to reconstruct from various sources what the 'lost ending' of this document may have said about Moses and Satan and the dispute over the body. The original story was clearly based on Scripture but included other details. Moses died before entering the Promised Land. God used the archangel Michael to bury Moses in some unknown place. Satan, however, with his usual malice and antagonism towards God's people,

---

13. Bauckham, R., *Jude, 2 Peter*, Word Biblical Commentary, 1983.

accused Moses of being a dreadful sinner for murdering
an Egyptian and therefore sought to deny Moses a proper
burial. This slanderous accusation was made before
Michael who, instead of rebuking Satan himself,
responded by saying to Satan: 'The Lord rebuke you!'
When Satan finally left, Michael took the body and
buried it in a place that no one knows.

The story may be somewhat alien to us, but in verse 10 Jude
now drives the message home with mounting scorn: **Yet these
men speak abusively against whatever they do not
understand**. His repeated use of **These men** (verses 12, 14,
16, 19) picks up on **these dreamers** of verse 8. They 'slander'
anything they do not understand. Instead of being the highly
spiritual people they think they are, they actually have no
spiritual understanding. They do indeed have some understanding, but what little they have is simply 'natural' and
limited to physical experiences: **and what things they do
understand** [they do so] **by instinct, like unreasoning
animals** –
    It is a sad fact that many people throughout history have
claimed to have spiritual insights and have often led people
astray, when actually they have nothing except the experience
of following their instincts. Instincts bring them closer to the
world of **unreasoning animals ('brute beasts')** than the
world of the Spirit and the things of God. In verse 19 Jude
reaches the climax of his devastating criticism of these so-
called 'spiritual' people by again saying that they follow
natural instincts and **do not have the Spirit**.
    Here is the key to the problem. These men do not possess
the Holy Spirit. They may claim to follow Christ but they do
not possess that all-important marker of the true Christian,
the Holy Spirit. Thus they were completely unable to discern
God's way and his truth. The apostle Paul recognises just the
same sort of problem among many who claim to be Christian

leaders in 1 Corinthians 2:14: 'the man without the Spirit does not accept the things that come from the Spirit of God, for they are foolishness to him, and he cannot understand them, because they are spiritually discerned.' That passage actually helps us understand things a little more clearly here in Jude. The problem, Paul notes, is that only the Holy Spirit actually knows the thoughts of God (verse 11), so if we want to claim to know the thoughts of God or spiritual matters that come from God then we must have the Spirit, and we receive the Spirit through faith in Christ.

So, having pointed out that these people actually do not know spiritual things but rather follow their animal instincts, Jude argues that **these are the very things that destroy them!** Sexual behaviour that is based upon animal instinct rather than the revelation of God carries with it the direct danger of destruction through illness, infection, etc. It is to this that Paul is surely referring in Romans 1:27. Here, however, Jude is more likely referring to the judgment and destruction to be faced at Christ's return.

Following the way of Christ and of the Spirit leads to eternal life and following our natural instincts, following the sins of Sodom and Gomorrah, and taking the way of Cain, Balaam and Korah will lead to the same destruction. These are the examples that Jude now uses to pursue his point.

Woe to them! They have taken the way of Cain; they have rushed for profit into Balaam's error; they have been destroyed in Korah's rebellion.

The first comparison Jude made revealed their total lack of spiritual understanding. The second comparison indicates even more clearly how evil **they** were.

b) Compare their behaviour with that of Cain, Balaam and Korah (verse 11)

Jude's comparison contains another set of three examples and begins with a strong condemnation in words used by Old Testament prophets and by Jesus: **Woe to them!** Jude's readers would have taken special note here at such strong language, for this is the language of cursing, of warning of final judgment by God (e.g. Isaiah 3:9, 11; Jeremiah 23:1). Jesus had called down woes upon the cities of Korazin and Bethsaida in Matthew 11:21 and the apostle Paul had called down a curse upon his own head using these words in 1 Corinthians 9:16 should he ever turn away from preaching the gospel of Christ.

The evil leaders **have taken the way of...**, in other words they have followed in the behaviour of the three men of history to which Jude now refers. Each of these actually did come under God's judgment. The lesson for Jude's audience is clear. These three – Cain, Balaam and Korah – were judged and condemned by God; the unspiritual leaders have followed the same direction and the same end awaits them, so to whom should this audience really listen and whom should they follow?

Cain killed his brother in a fit of jealousy and rage that emanated from his lack of faith. In Genesis 4 we read that Cain and his brother Abel brought 'offerings' to God. Cain brought fruit and Abel brought 'fat portions from some of the first born of his flock' (verses 3-4). 'The Lord looked with favour on Abel and his offering', but did not do so on Cain's. There is no indication why God distinguished between the two in this way, but in v 5 we read that Cain was angry and depressed, so God challenged him about this reaction and pointed out that his offering would be acceptable if he did 'what is right'. The implication of God's comments with his mention of 'sin ... crouching at your door .... you must master it' (verse 7) is that the Lord, who looks on the heart, knew that Cain's heart was sinful. Cain's subsequent action confirms that impression. He was angry against both God and his brother. Hebrews 11:4 supports this view of Cain and his behaviour, for the writer there distinguishes between Cain and Abel on the grounds of the faith that Abel showed and that was lacking in Cain.

Cain's actions were perhaps the inevitable outcome of his lack of faith. Lack of faith had led to a lack of love and caring for his brother and to great jealousy, rage and eventually murder. This would be the end of **these men** with whom Jude is concerned. They too were headed the same way following **their own evil desires** (verse 16).

The second example is Balaam. **They have rushed for profit into Balaam's error.** Balaam seems at first to be a strange example as he received genuine communications from God and, at least to begin with, stood against accepting bribes (Numbers 22:1-20). Balak, king of the Moabites, wanted Balaam to curse the Israelites who were beginning to take over the land. Balaam refused to do so. Eventually, Balaam did go to Balak, but only prophesied what the Lord God told him and, rather than putting a curse on the Israelites, he blessed them (Numbers 23-24). Balak did not like this at all, and eventually Balaam returned home. In Numbers 25 the narrative moves immediately to describing how the Israelites were seduced to worship other gods and to become involved in sexual promiscuity with the Moabites. Although Numbers 23-24 tells us nothing of Balaam's part in this seduction of Israel, we read in Numbers 31 that Balaam had urged this course of action on the Moabites (31:8, 16). Thousands of Israelites were judged for their sin, immorality and pagan worship. In Revelation 2:14 Jesus, writing to the church at Pergamum, refers to people who hold the same teaching as Balaam who enticed 'the Israelites to sin by eating food sacrificed to idols and by committing sexual immorality'.

This, no doubt, is the example to which Jude is referring. Just as Balaam, for the sake of personal gain, wanted to see God's people destroyed and was able to lead many astray so that they were judged, so **these men**, seeking only **their own advantage** (verse 16) were drawing the people of God into serious sin and leading them towards the inevitable end: judgment.

they have been destroyed in Korah's rebellion – introduces us to the third Old Testament illustration, this time from Numbers 16:1-35. Korah, a leader in the tribe of Levi, led a rebellion against Moses. Again for Jude's purposes the illustration is relevant because it is an example of ungodly leaders standing up against God's own leader and his revealed truth and rapidly receiving the judgment of God. In Numbers 16:31-35 we find that all those who had followed Korah were swallowed up and destroyed by the opening of the ground, while those involved in illegal sacrifices were consumed by fire. The picture of devastation would not be lost on Jude's readers. The message of all three examples is this: compare your leaders with other godless, immoral leaders who were judged – look at what happened under Cain, Balaam and Korah.

Jude now moves to the final part of this comparison. **These men** have been compared unfavourably with the archangel Michael. They have been compared favourably with evil leaders of the past who seduced and corrupted God's people and were finally destroyed by God. Now in a third main comparison Jude suggests that the reader should

c) Compare their behaviour with aspects of nature (verses 12-13)

These men are blemishes at your love feasts, eating with you without the slightest qualm – shepherds who feed only themselves. They are clouds without rain, blown along by the wind; autumn trees, without fruit and uprooted – twice dead.

They are wild waves of the sea, foaming up their shame; wandering stars, for whom blackest darkness has been reserved for ever.

Here the emphasis is on the emptiness of all that they are and say, the perversity of their hypocrisy and the horror of their end. Jude uses devastatingly simply pictures that all of us understand well.

... shepherds who feed only themselves. The job of any shepherd is to look after his sheep. Sheep die if they are not fed properly or looked after. These people are among the leaders of this church and have 'slipped in' without people really noting what has happened. In some ways they probably seem rather nice leaders. They encourage fun. They speak against the law. Their teachings are quite attractive and have a semblance of godliness to them. But instead of feeding the flock, they feed only themselves.

The picture of the leader of God's people as a 'shepherd' goes right back into the earliest times. Abraham looked after flocks of sheep and other animals and Moses was a shepherd. But the most famous was King David who was anointed to be king of Israel while still only a shepherd boy. Later the prophets warned about shepherds who were not shepherding God's people but rather taking advantage of their position to look after themselves. So bad was the situation that God said he would have to take over the shepherding directly and so promised to replace all the evil leaders of Israel: 'Woe to the shepherds of Israel who only take care of themselves! Should not shepherds take care of the flock?... As a shepherd looks after his scattered flock when he is with them, so will I look after my sheep .... I myself will tend my sheep and make them lie down, declares the Sovereign Lord' (Ezekiel 34:2, 11-15). God had judged the evil leaders of his people before, and he would do so again. Those of Jude's day were just like those of old, and God would intervene.

They are blemishes at your love feasts reminds us that these leaders were sitting down in fellowship with the very flock they were leading astray. These love feasts were probably meals held in the early church to encourage love and care and fellowship among Christians (1 Corinthians 11:20-22). They may have been related to what we call a 'communion service' except that they were full meals and not just a matter of taking a small portion of bread and a sip of wine. Here was a focus of what true fellowship was all about, a situation in which the leaders were to sit down with their flock, encouraging them and building them up in the faith, exhorting them to believe the truth of the gospel and to keep the law of Christ. But none of this was happening. This focal part of the Christian community's activity was becoming just another opportunity for selfish feasting, for licentiousness, and for carousing. At the very point where the love and unity of the community should most clearly be seen, these leaders were disobeying God, rejecting all authority and living by animal instincts. Is it any wonder they are regarded as **blemishes**.

Four lessons from nature now follow.

They are clouds without rain, blown along by the wind. This is a vivid picture of their deception. In a climate where water is often desperately needed, the large dark clouds that sometimes blow up are eagerly anticipated. At last rain will come. The greatest frustration for the farmer who needs water to produce good crops is when the clouds come and go but there is no life-giving rain. This is the way false teachers all the way down through the ages have deceived God's people, and it happens as much today. Those who sit light to God's word are just like this. Those who would lead us in other directions and suggest to congregations committed to their care that there is no need to follow Scripture and the word of God, in fact provide nothing which increases growth or brings life to God's people. Time and again modern churches suffer from just this suggestion of great things that fail to materialise. How often we see leaders who are dynamic in their leadership, who promise much, who have an appearance of wisdom and love and care, and yet, when we look beneath the surface, have nothing to offer. Such people will never help a congregation to grow in their knowledge and love of the Lord, but will rather fill the space with other things that promise much but deliver little. Just as clouds are blown away from the place that most needs the rain, so these false teachers have been blown off course and have nothing of value for anyone. The picture of wind and waterless clouds is again one drawn from the Old Testament. Proverbs 25:14 says: 'Like clouds and wind without rain is a man who boasts of gifts he does not give.'

autumn trees, without fruit and uprooted – twice dead. This second picture adds still more to the picture of doom associated with such leaders. The leaders are like trees that promised to bear fruit but in fact never did. For fruit farmers such trees are useless and simply take up valuable ground. They have to be uprooted and burnt on the fire. **twice dead** probably means that they were dead in the sense of having no fruit but also dead because they were then uprooted. However, in the Book of Revelation the idea of a second death relates to the final judgment (2:11; 20:6; 21:8) and it is likely that Jude has this in mind here. Such leaders will not only be uprooted and die a first time (physically) but they will be judged to eternal death as well.

They are wild waves of the sea, foaming up their shame. Nothing is more unpredictable than the great stormy seas that crash on rocky coastlines around the world. Storms and gales produce dangerous waves that will all too easily sweep people away. There is a sense that the sea is completely uncontrollable. The best of sea defences eventually break down after repeated storms. The ferocity of the sea has become a by-word for danger. As these wild waves hit the shore so they produce a foam generated from the pollution of the water and from the effects of the waves in breaking down the coastline. These false and evil teachers are as dangerous and as out of control as the wildest of seas. The foam produced by the waves provides a vivid picture of the cesspool produced by their shameful conduct. If the picture brings to mind real fear, so it should. The greatest protection for this congregation and Christians down through the ages, is to be fearful of all who might lead them astray. Just as fear of the sea is healthy when the storms rage, so it is right that Christians should keep a wary eye out, fearful lest they should be led astray by such people and find that shipwreck is the only possible outcome. Again the Old Testament provides Jude with this illustration. In Isaiah 57:20 we read: 'But the wicked are like the tossing sea, which cannot rest, whose waves cast up mire and mud.'

The final example of Jude's last main comparison is again easily understood. These men are **like wandering stars, for whom blackest darkness has been reserved for ever**. In ancient times the planets were the stars which wandered around, as opposed to those which appeared to be fixed in space. Indeed the word 'planet' comes from the word here meaning 'wandering' (*planao*). 'Error' (verse 11) comes from the same word. To 'wander' is to 'err'. The false leaders, then, seem like those stars which cannot be relied upon properly to guide the traveller. For these, the teachers, the blackest darkness has been reserved for ever. This recalls verse 6 and the judgment on the angels who fell from grace. Indeed in the book of Enoch, which is quoted in verse 14, the stars which go astray are linked to the fallen angels. Here it is more likely that Jude is simply driving home yet again the destiny of **these men**. In the parable of the talents Jesus himself had talked of 'darkness' being reserved for the worthless servant who had produced nothing (Matthew 25:30). This is precisely Jude's point. Eternal separation from the light of God awaits those who reject his light in this life.

5. Their judgment was predicted (verses 14-19)
Having shown how these insidious leaders behave so differently from the archangel Michael, and how similar their behaviour is to that of rebellious leaders of the past like Cain, Balaam and Korah, and having demonstrated that they have nothing but deceitful lies to offer anyone and that their judgment is already sealed, Jude now moves on to argue that all this was prophesied beforehand. First, there was the prophecy of Enoch (verses 14-16) and then, even more significantly, the apostles themselves had foretold the coming of such ungodly people (verses 17-19).

a) Enoch's prophecy
Enoch, the seventh from Adam, prophesied about these men ... Jude used the past tense in verse 13 to affirm the ultimate destruction of these men. The certainty of judgment for the ungodly is so clear in Scripture and is prophesied so clearly that Jude can speak of it as if it had already happened. He had done the same back in verse 11 where he said: **they have been destroyed in Korah's rebellion**. Their fate is sealed. Indeed church members reading this letter would realise that just the same judgment for the ungodly was promised in a book with which they were very familiar, the Book of Enoch. (See Appendix on the use of this book.)

Jude does not necessarily understand this prophecy to be 'inspired' in the way we accept Holy Scripture as inspired. Rather Jude is concerned to pick up on the predictive element of what Enoch said. The concept of 'prophecy' used in this way is not unknown in Scripture. The apostle Paul referred

to a Cretan as 'one of their own prophets' and then proceeded
to quote him, adapting the message to make his own particular
point (Titus 1:12). Jude adapts Enoch, drawing on the
prophecy i) that God would return with his angels to judge;
and ii) that all ungodly sinners will be convicted. The
repetition of the words 'all' and 'ungodly' is noticeable here.

Jude's readers had a high regard for the Book of Enoch
and so this citation adds evidence to the truth of Jude's
message. Several aspects of what Jude says here are worth
noting.

First, it is Christ who will judge. Jude adapts Enoch 1:9 to
emphasise the role of Jesus Christ in this judgment. **See, the
Lord is coming** (verse 14). Instead of God being the one
who will come, as in Enoch, for Jude it is 'the Lord', that is
Jesus Christ. The judgment of these evil people is therefore
to be made final with the return of the Lord Jesus.

It was characteristic of the early New Testament churches
that they lived very much in the light of the return of Christ.
In most of the epistles there are appeals to remember Christ's
return, or to live in readiness of his return. In other cases the
return of Christ is held up as a comfort to the persecuted.
This teaching is sometimes all but ignored in the modern
church and yet should be fundamental to who we are and
how we live in and think about our world. Here Jude uses the
fact of Christ's return to remind the congregation that false
teachers will eventually face the same judgment that
'everyone' will face. Their end, their condemnation, has been
decreed in advance. It is a sombre warning, but one the modern
church would do well to heed as we are all too ready to tolerate
all sorts of unbiblical teachers. To tolerate falsehood in the
church is to acquiesce in it, so we too need to hear the warning
inherent in knowing Christ will return. Equally, though, for
those who remain faithful and, as a result, often suffer at the
hands of those who teach 'another Gospel', the doctrine of

Christ's return is one that should bring us great comfort for, on that Day, the Lord will vindicate his name and his people.

Second, Christ will return **with thousands upon thousands** *of his holy ones*. That angels will accompany Christ's return was taught by Christ himself and also picks up on a number of Old Testament prophecies. In Matthew 25:31 we read: 'When the Son of Man comes in his glory, and all the angels with him, he will sit on his throne in heavenly glory' (see also Daniel 7:10). But in the Old Testament the most interesting parallel is found in Deuteronomy 33:2 where Moses pronounces a blessing on the Israelites reminding them of God's appearance to them on Mount Sinai, and the fact that the giving of the Law was accompanied by the presence of angels: 'The LORD came from Sinai and dawned over them from Seir; he shone forth from Mount Paran. He came with myriads of holy ones ...'[14] There is a great double irony here in Jude: the very law the teachers so despised was put into effect through the angels whose authority they slandered (verse 8), and it is these very angels, so despised by the false teachers, who will be present at their judgment.

Third, everyone will be judged. **the Lord is coming ... to judge everyone.** Perhaps the false teachers were claiming there was to be no judgment or at the very least they and their followers would not have to worry about this. This is the teaching of many church leaders today. It has always been one of the more unpalatable parts of biblical teaching that God will return to judge. Human beings have never liked the thought that someone stands above and beyond them and that they will have to answer to that person one day, but that is how God has dealt with us. He made us to be responsible human beings and revealed himself to us as a God who comes to us in love and with promise of blessing if we worship him

14. Angels are further linked with the giving of the Sinai law and its implementation in Acts 7:38, 53; Galatians 3:19; Hebrews 2:2.

and obey his covenant. But he will also hold us responsible if we reject his covenant, rebel against him and despise his Law, and his teaching. In his great mercy and grace, the covenant Lord continued to pour out his blessing by being prepared to forgive his people as they sinned, and then eventually by even sending his own Son to take his people's sin upon himself on the cross, to die in their place. Nevertheless, those who are not prepared to accept that gift of love, and who continue to reject his covenant Lordship know their end is certain, for judgment awaits.

This was the message of Deuteronomy 30:19-20 where the LORD laid before his people life and death, blessings and curses. The appeal was obvious: 'Choose life, so that you and your children may live and that you may love the LORD your God, listen to his voice, and hold fast to him. For the LORD is your life ...' This was the message of the prophets and then the message of Jesus himself. As Lord of the covenant, Jesus focused the issue on himself (John 5:24): 'I tell you the truth, whoever hears my word and believes him who sent me has eternal life and will not be condemned; he has crossed over from death to life.'

In our churches today we are faced with the same truths. Unless we commit ourselves to the one and only covenant Lord Jesus and to his word, then we shall stand under the same condemnation that Jude insists faces the teachers he is dealing with, for *everyone will be judged.*

Fourth, conviction awaits the ungodly. The word 'ungodly' occurs four times in verse 15. We have already seen in verse 4 how the word is used to summarise the evil of the wicked infiltrators. It will be repeated one last time in verse 18. Here the repetition is deliberate. Thus when the Lord returns he will **convict all the ungodly of all the ungodly acts they have done in the ungodly way, and of all the harsh words ungodly sinners have spoken against him**. It is in verse 16 that the specifics of at least some of their ungodliness is spelled out. But much of it has already been noted in verses 4, 8, 12-13 etc. The word summarises these people and their behaviour. These are people who are disobeying the will of God and whose actions reveal a rejection of God's authority.

There will be no doubt on that final judgment day of the justice of the sentence when the Lord reveals just how ungodly these people have been in their immorality, their licentiousness and denial of the Lord Jesus as Master (verse 4), and in their deceit and selfish ambitions (verses 12-13). Their conviction will be altogether just.

Fifth, ungodly people can be identified. Jude is writing to warn normal Christian people in a church where the ungodly seem to have infiltrated at all levels. While these people have 'secretly slipped in among' the church (verse 4) and could have hardly got as far as they have if they had worn placards on their arms, nevertheless, Jude insists that with some care and attention it should be possible to identify them.

There is a contrast between godly men and women and those whom Jude confronts. Verse 16 makes this clear as Jude continues to talk of their ungodliness. **These men are grumblers and fault-finders; they follow their own evil desires; they boast about themselves and flatter others for their own advantage**. For those who are aware of the problem, it is this lack of godliness which will help identify wolves who appear in sheep's clothing. Just as Jesus once warned against false prophets and said, 'by their fruit you shall know them' (Matthew 7:16), so here Jude points out the same truth. Deceit is not always easy to see through. Subtle changes of doctrine in, say, destroying the grace of God into a licence for immorality, may not always be obviously wrong if careful arguments are brought to bear for the changes. However, true leaders of Christ's church should be marked out by godliness of character and their godly actions.

It is easy to understand immorality as ungodly behaviour. We see the more spectacular sins and readily recognise that sort of ungodly behaviour, but Jude is here helping us learn to recognise evil people not through the obvious and big sins of life, but through what many might consider rather trivial. Yet these apparently trivial matters are, throughout Scripture, a touchstone for identifying the difference between the godly and the ungodly. **Grumblers and fault finders** are so commonly found in churches that it hardly seems worth mentioning in such a serious discussion as Jude is having. Nevertheless, Jude has already mentioned in verse 5 how warnings should be taken from the wilderness generation of the Israelites. Their greatest sin, referred to many times through the Old Testament, was the sin of grumbling against the Lord and his servant Moses. They found fault with Moses and with God for bringing them out of Egypt into a wilderness. They grumbled at not having enough food. Indeed there were ten major occasions when the Israelites were judged for their 'grumbling'. The Greek word used here is also the word used in the Greek version of the Old Testament (the LXX). The link is hardly to be disputed. Drawing yet again on the Old Testament for lessons for today's church, Jude reminds true people of faith and trust, that good and godly leaders do not grumble and find fault with God's way forward and his rule for life.

Instead of following God, these men **follow their own evil desires**. Just like those who rebelled in the Israelite community in the wilderness, these people are more interested in their own easier ways of living and their ungodliness becomes clear to all in their rebellion. **They boast about themselves and flatter others for their own advantage**. These are the characteristics of those who are ungodly, no matter how persuasive they sound or how nice they appear on the surface.

Special Lessons for Today

How much stronger our churches would be these days if
people would recognise that grumbling and fault-finding are
an indication of an *ungodly* life. Perhaps we would more
quickly dissociate ourselves from such groups or people who
lead such cliques, if we realised the seriousness of what Jude
is saying here. Too often people are encouraged to join the
grumblers and those who are leading in fault-finding simply
because they are being flattered and made to feel good.

Discernment is also a greatly needed gift in the modern
church. It is vital to realise that it is possible to discern even
the cleverest, most flattering of deceitful people in a church
by looking at their ungodly life-style and their ungodly
actions. The mark of a godly leader will be the opposite. He
will lead the flock to obey the will of God, and will encourage
and build them up in the faith and the ways of the Lord rather
than grumble and find fault. Perhaps if the faithful leaders of
our churches were more obviously godly in their way of life
the contrast with others would be the more noticeable.

The knowledge that 'the Lord is coming' ought to keep
the whole church on its toes, but compromise, lack of clarity
in doctrine and biblical behaviour have led to a general
complacency in the modern church. Christ is reduced to the
parts we like or that are acceptable to 'the itching ears' that
will only listen to what they want to hear (2 Timothy 4:3).
The Christ who returns to judge is ignored. The Christ who
differentiates between the godly and the ungodly is rarely
mentioned. The Christ who will not tolerate false teaching
and will return with myriads of angels is a myth of the past.

The choice that lies before individual Christians and the
church at large is the same today as it was for Jude's times:
the end of the ungodly and of those who teach falsely is certain
– where do we stand? Are we ready for Christ's return or do
we tolerate that which will stand condemned on the Last Day?

b) The apostles' predictions (verses 17-19)

Enoch, one of the writers who would have been well known among Jude's congregation, had prophesied that the Lord would return and that false teachers would be judged and convicted. Such teaching of judgment was, as Jude has shown, a natural and reasonable understanding of Old Testament Scripture. Jude used Enoch, therefore, to warn the false teachers of their impending doom. But now Jude turns to the true believers in the church and reminds them of another vital prophecy if they are to be properly prepared for the world in which they now find themselves seeking to keep the faith.

The apostles themselves had prophesied a message that all Christians need to hear: false teachers will come into the church, and they will cause divisions. **But, dear friends, remember what the apostles of our Lord Jesus Christ foretold**.

Jude returns in these last verses of his epistle to being the affectionate pastor who is so concerned for God's faithful people in this church. He has warned the false teachers and spelled out clearly from Scripture what their end is to be, but now he comforts and encourages and seeks to build up the faithful believers. **But you ...** These faithful brothers and sisters in Christ cannot sit idly by even if the false teachers will eventually be judged by God. Here he picks up again on what he had said in verse 3 – they must 'earnestly contend for the faith that was once for all entrusted to the saints'.

These people 'loved in God the Father' (verse 1) are again 'loved' by Jude, as in verses 3 and 20 (**dear friends**, NIV).[15] As part of the once and for all delivered faith the apostles had made this startling prophecy and it must now guide their thinking and their actions: **They said**[16] **to you, 'In the last**

---

15. The Greek means 'loved' or 'beloved'. The verbal form is used in verse 1 and the noun form in verses 3, 17, 20.

16. 'They said' is here in the imperfect tense in Greek. This suggests that it was an oft repeated warning from the apostles.

times there will be scoffers who will follow their own
ungodly desires.'

Remember... With the first of five commands in the last
few verses of his epistle, Jude insists that the teachings of the
apostles are foundational and must be recalled if these
Christians are to survive and not to be led astray themselves
by false teaching. Clearly on many occasions the apostles
must have taught about false teachers and their danger. In
doing this they were, of course, passing on what Jesus had
taught them. In Mark 13:22-23 Jesus had warned: 'For false
Christs and false prophets will appear and perform signs and
miracles to deceive the elect – if that were possible. So be on
your guard; I have told you everything ahead of time.' Jesus
had prophesied this, and the apostles had carried forward that
prophecy into the next generation and into the young church.
The apostle Paul provides just one of many examples of this
when he spoke to the Ephesian elders in Acts 20:29-31: 'I
know that after I leave, savage wolves will come in among
you and will not spare the flock. Even from your own number
men will arise and distort the truth in order to draw away
disciples after them. So be on your guard!' If Jude knew 2
Peter then perhaps he specifically had in mind Peter's own
prediction of 2 Peter 2:1, but it is more likely a general
reference to many apostolic warnings.

The church of all generations has been called by Jesus and
the apostles to 'be on guard!' Jude commands his people to
'remember' this, just as we today need to remember the pre-
dictions of Christ and the apostles. What we must remember
is that the existence of these people, these 'scoffers', and self-
centred leaders, is part and parcel of the age in which we
live: **the last times**. In the New Testament the 'last times'
refers to the period between the first coming of Jesus leading
up to his return in glory.[17] Like Jude and his congregation,

---

17. In 2 Timothy 3:1 Paul warns about the 'terrible times' to be experienced

we live in the 'last times' or 'last days' and so this prophecy
must remain foundational for our approach to our own situation at the start of the twenty-first century.

Jesus, the apostles and Jude all knew that the recognition
of this simple fact was the first step to dealing with the
situation. The command to 'remember' is therefore deeply
significant for all of us. If people seem to be nice enough,
and to teach at least something about the Lord Jesus then we
are too easily able to forgive what are literally 'a multitude
of sins'. It is not enough to speak of the love of the Lord
Jesus and then to encourage people to sit loose to the words
of Jesus, or to permit the practice of immorality, or to
encourage selfish behaviour. Jude talks of **scoffers**, and this
is more than simply a reference to those who might poke fun
at us. Scoffers here refers to those who think they know better
and so pour scorn on other Christians. They 'scoff' at those
who perhaps have what may be called a 'simple' faith. We
see scoffers like this in the present who scoff at those who
take the Bible to be the infallible Word of God. They scoff at
those who say that we need to live by the Bible as God's
Word. They scoff when Christians seek to apply the Bible to
the world around them and to judge their own behaviour and
the behaviour of others in the light of Scripture.

The attack on the plain apostolic teaching of Scripture,
the attempt to suggest that Jesus could not have said some of
the more 'unpalatable' teachings attributed to him in
Scripture, the attempt to argue that much of what we know
about Jesus, was added by an overzealous early church, are
all ways in which false teachers 'have secretly slipped in
among us'. As Jude said to his people and as he speaks to us

---

in the last days. In 1 Peter 1:20 Peter talks of the revelation of Christ 'in
these last days'. But 'the last day' can also refer quite specifically to the day
of final judgment as in John 12:48. The concept has its origins in the Old
Testament in which the last day is both the day of salvation and of judgment
(e.g. Isaiah 2:2; Hosea 3:5).

in God's Word across the generations: it is time, dear friends,
for us to remember just what the apostles taught concerning
these things. To be fore-warned is to be fore-armed. But before
continuing to show how best we should arm ourselves, Jude
has one last summary description of 'these men' in verse 19.

**These are the men who divide you, who follow mere
natural instincts and do not have the Spirit**. It is vital that
they realise that **these are the men** who are the ones the
apostles spoke about. The identification is certain. In yet
another list of three, Jude summarises who they are. The Greek
can be translated like this: 'these are the ones who make
distinctions, who are worldly, and who do not have the Spirit.'
Of course, Jude is saying little more than he has said
throughout the letter about these evil people, and yet perhaps
he highlights here something that has not really been clear to
this point. The word translated 'make distinctions' refers to
more than simply causing divisions (NIV). It is a rare word in
Greek and seems to imply classifying people into groups.
Given the point that Jude then makes that they are 'worldly'
and 'devoid of the Spirit', it is surely likely that these people
were making the same mistake highlighted by the apostle
Paul in 1 Corinthians. They regarded themselves as 'spiritual'
and others as 'worldly'. They made distinctions within the
church, putting themselves on a higher plane than others. This
would fit well with Jude's comments in verse 12 that they
'feed only themselves' and in verse 16 that they 'boast about
themselves and flatter others for their own advantage'.

As Paul showed so clearly in 1 Corinthians (specially in
chapter 2:14-15 where he contrasts 'spiritual' people with
'worldly' – using the same Greek word *psykikoi* – 'the man
without the Spirit', NIV), it is completely wrong to make
distinctions between Christians. There is no higher order of
the spiritual as opposed to the others. Rather there are those
who are real Christians, those who belong to Christ and have

the Spirit (Romans 8:9), and those who do not have the Spirit and therefore, in spite of their protestations to the contrary do not actually belong to the Lord.

Jude here is saying that it is in fact these men who are worldly and devoid of the Spirit. They are making distinctions, but they have got it entirely the wrong way round. They have no part in the true church, for they do not have the Spirit. Indeed they are 'godless' (verse 4).

Other Lessons for Today

One of the saddest aspects of church life, even as we often experience it today, is that those who lead people astray end up causing divisions among people as they draw people after themselves, rather than pointing them to the Lord. It is worth remembering as we seek to discern those who would ultimately tear apart our churches, that one of the evidences of the Holy Spirit's presence in our leaders will be their continuing attempt to bring about a unity of the body of Christ based not on themselves but on the revealed truth to be found in Jesus and in the Holy Scriptures. Those who do not seek this unity in Christ and his truth have a worldly agenda and, no matter how plausible may seem their arguments, we need to 'remember what the apostles of our Lord Jesus Christ foretold'.

Some churches in recent years have been faced with people who seem to undermine the work of a church by claiming they are more 'spiritual' or are 'closer to God' than fellow Christians. Instead of seeking to build others up in the faith or encouraging the chosen leadership in the church, they grumble, and cause divisions between good Christian people. Often their emphasis is on experience. They 'flatter themselves' and urge others to become like them rather than become more Christ-like. The centrality of the message of Christ crucified is compromised or even lost.

It is possible to apply the idea of 'following their **natural instincts**' in a general way. Do we follow our own instincts and natural inclinations or do we follow the Spirit and what God wants of us? But Jude's meaning is more specific, for he is talking of immoral behaviour. Sadly, here too we can make some obvious applications. The church faces numerous serious moral challenges. For example, a number of people now argue that some are genetically (i.e. 'by nature') homosexually inclined. They go on to suggest that, if this is the case, then it is quite wrong to prohibit practising homosexual relationships provided they are 'faithful' friendships. The ordination of practising homosexuals, of people who have been adulterous etc. is also on the agenda for discussion in some denominations. However, whether or not some sexual tendencies are genetic surely has little to do with God's law and our need to obey the Master. It is indeed part of our 'nature' as sinful human beings to desire sin. We cannot use 'nature' or genetics as excuses for disobeying God's commands.

However, let us be careful never to regard ourselves as better than others in this for we are all 'by nature' fallen and sinful, but as forgiven sinners let us strive to build a church that remembers the apostolic warnings and seeks to live in a godly manner among 'a crooked and perverse generation' (Philippians 2:15). Let us seek God's protection as we identify and then stand against those who would divide Christians and lead them astray.

6. Jude's summary and appeal for urgent precautions (verses 20-23)

But you, dear friends (exactly the same Greek and therefore the same emphasis as at the start of verse 17), **build yourselves up in your most holy faith.**

a) Protect yourselves (verses 20-21)

Jude's second command, **build yourselves up ...**, indicates
his move now to giving some distinctly practical advice for
the true believers in this church. It is essential that these
Christian believers not be carried away into error, so they
must take precautions. The first of these is to make sure they
are firmly established in their most holy faith.

In the previous verse we noted there were strong parallels
between what the false teachers were doing in this church
and the problems Paul faced at Corinth. Jude's first
exhortation to the believers is also deeply reminiscent of
Paul's epistle, where the concept of 'being built up' figures
prominently. The church is God's building, built on the
foundation of Jesus Christ (e.g. 1 Corinthians 3:9-11; 8:1;
14:12 etc.). In that sense God does the building. **Your most
holy faith** refers to the whole of that gospel truth, the whole
once and for all delivered faith mentioned in verse 3. At its
heart we can sum it up as the belief in Christ crucified – not
simply in some credal form, important as that is, but a belief
in Christ which is life-changing.

Since the church is God's building, built on Christ, loved
by God and fully dependent upon his grace for all that it is, it
can sound strange that in this command and those which
follow, Jude emphasises the church's own work rather than
the truths of God's keeping and protecting grace that he
mentioned back in verses 1-2. It is thus important to
understand both what Jude is and what he is *not* saying here.
He is *not* saying that the survival of these Christians as true
believers is dependent upon their ability to have faith or (verse
21) their ability to love God properly or (verse 22) their ability
to have mercy. Their survival as God's people is dependent
upon grace alone. We noted in verse 1 how Jude used the
past tense when he spoke of them as 'called by God', 'the
loved by God' and the ones 'kept by Jesus Christ'. These are

the ones who *do* have the Holy Spirit, in contrast with those who do not (verse 19). Indeed, in verses 24-25, as we shall see, Jude returns to this underlying foundational truth that it is ultimately only God who can 'keep his people from falling and present them faultless before his glorious presence'. So what is Jude driving at when he says, 'build yourselves up in your ... faith'?

First, we need to note that 'the faith' is indeed the proclamation of Christ who died for our sins and who calls us all to repentance.

Second, we must note that the faith is 'most holy', that is, it is set apart, it is from God himself. Anything to do with God is described as 'holy' and this faith comes from God himself. It is not therefore a subjective personal faith that Jude is talking of here. Rather he is calling them back to that which is revealed, the 'given-ness' of Christianity.

Third, the call to 'build yourselves up' is addressed in this context to all those who are true believers. It is an appeal to the church, the body of Christ, to work together in this process of commitment to and study of the truth revealed first in the Christ of Scripture.

If we now put this together we see immediately that Jude's command is to the whole church to study and to be involved in working out how to live and move on in life with the grace of God revealed in Jesus. It is not about an individual's salvation, but about the church, loved by God and called by him, being absorbed with what God has given. A healthy church that is able to stand against falsehood will be a church in which the people are committed to the given-ness of the faith, to Christ, to Scripture as the word of God, and to each other as the body of Christ. God's people will seek to show themselves approved of God and to be workmen who do not need to be ashamed for they correctly handle the word of truth (2 Timothy 2:15). The apostle Paul sums up the message of Jude's command in Colossians 2:6-7 when he says: 'So then, just as you received Christ Jesus as Lord, continue to live in him, ... strengthened in the faith as you were taught, and overflowing with thankfulness.'

In today's world where often the church is encouraged to base its behaviour and teaching upon subjective experiences of individuals, we need to hear again this call to return to the given-ness of the faith, to the 'holiness' of that faith, its separateness and its origin not in us and our feelings but in God and his revelation. It is commitment to that once and for all delivered faith, that will protect us and enable us to test those who come claiming to have special personal revelations from God and claiming to have some 'deeper' level of spirituality that in fact is no spirituality.

Our faith must be held personally and our commitment to it must be felt from the bottom of our hearts. It must be life-changing and it must be something we long to share with others. But the subjective and experiential side of what we believe needs to be subordinated to the 'set apart once delivered faith' to which we are committed. As we study this and build ourselves up in this faith so we will find ourselves protected by God from those who would oppose the gospel truth, but so also we will find that our personal commitment to Christ and our experience of the reality of the Lord who loves us becomes ever more real.

Even though we are called upon to build ourselves up in our most holy faith, we are not, of course, left alone in this. The faith comes from God. It is a gift of God to his church and applied to our lives by his Spirit. As Luther once put it: 'Faith is the foundation on which one should build. But to build up means to increase from day to day in the knowledge of God and of Jesus Christ. This is done through the Holy Spirit.'[18] And so Jude moves to the third command.

---

18. Martin Luther, *Works*, Vol. 30, p. 214.

Pray in the Holy Spirit. The need for earnest and continuing prayer is vital if believers are to stand properly against those who would lead them astray. Such prayer reflects dependence upon God for help and strength. Prayer 'in the Spirit' is a prominent thought in the apostle Paul's writings and no doubt the concept was well understood among those to whom Jude was writing. In Ephesians 6:18, also in a context of exhortation to stand against falsehood and the devil's schemes, Paul says: 'Pray in the Spirit on all occasions with all kinds of prayers and requests. With this in mind, ... always keep on praying for all the saints.'

As we pray, so the Holy Spirit, who is with God's people permanently, takes those prayers right into the presence of the Father.[19] How different are such prayers from those of the false teachers who do not have the Spirit (verse 19). Everything Jude is now saying contrasts directly with those who would have Christians believe they are somehow on a deeper spiritual plain when in fact they are nowhere spiritually. Romans 8:26-27 helps us understand this work of the Spirit in our prayer lives. It is surely the experience of every Christian that there are times when we do not even know how or what to pray for some situations. At times we are not even aware that we ought to be praying for particular protection from the evil one. Paul tells us that the Holy Spirit 'helps us in our weakness' when this happens to us. 'The Spirit himself intercedes for us'. But more than that, praying in the Holy Spirit allows us to be confident in the will of God himself being carried out in our lives. As we pray, we are aware that the Spirit knows the will of God and so bears us up and our needs up 'in accordance with the will of God'. The joy for all believers is that God hears and answers all such prayers brought to him in accordance with his will. What

19. There is no evidence here that Jude has in mind praying in tongues, or anything of the like, as some have suggested.

a joy to know that even when we are not aware of just what God's will may be, the Holy Spirit prays on our behalf.

Here, then, is yet another command that the modern church needs to hear just as much as the church of Jude's day. It is so sad that many of our churches find it so hard to get Christians to come together as a church for corporate prayer. The prayers of God's people as his church, prayers offered 'in the Spirit', are vital if people are not to be left open to the deceitful teachings of the heretics. Some churches have actually given up the church 'prayer meeting' as a lost cause, yet prayer is part of the spiritual battle in which we are engaged both as individuals and also *as a church*. How can we expect to be powerful in fulfilling the Lord's will in our local areas if as churches we do not come together and pray? Are we surprised that many churches have been led away from the truth by false teachers who pander to those who find it an uncomfortable discipline to turn out for a prayer meeting?

Let us thank God that in prayer we are perhaps most able to show our utter dependence upon God and his Spirit to help us survive and persevere as God's people.

Keep yourselves in God's love is Jude's fourth command, and continues his exhortation to his audience to protect themselves properly from falsehood. It reminds his readers that the covenant Lord and Master, who has called them, loved them and kept them (verse 1), asks for our love in response. God's electing, ever-faithful, covenant love for his people does not, however, leave us struggling to love as we should in response to his covenant. As with the need to pray, we must remember that the Holy Spirit has been given to us so that the law of love is now written on our hearts – the law to love God with all our heart and soul and mind and strength and our neighbour as ourselves.

Jude's command then must be read in the light of this total covenantal relationship. He is asking true believers to ensure

that they really live out in day to day life the reality of being
God's people. In practice this means obeying the commands
of God, unlike the false teachers who do not obey God's law.
In John 15:9-10 Jesus spoke clearly of this relationship
between the love of God for his people and their love for
him: 'As the Father has loved me so have I loved you. Now
remain in my love. If you obey my commands you will remain
in my love, just as I have obeyed my Father's commands and
remain in his love.'

Jude then reminds his readers of the context in which this
command is given, **as you wait for the mercy of our Lord
Jesus Christ to bring you to eternal life**. In these two verses
Jude has thus referred directly to two of the three abiding
Christian characteristics, faith and love, and now indirectly
he points to the third, hope (see 1 Corinthians 13:13). It is
vital for all Christians to remember they are living in an age
that will come to an end. The 'last times' (verse 18) do lead
on to the inevitable Last Day when this age will come to an
end and the 'full mercy of our Lord Jesus Christ' will be seen
as he brings us the fulfilment of the promise of 'eternal life'.
The life of the church and of individual Christians in the last
times will not be easy, as Jude has shown. But we are to
persevere with the help of the Holy Spirit, for that great and
glorious eternity awaits us when we shall see God's mercy
and salvation in all its fullness. At the moment we experience
it through faith and as the Spirit writes God's confirming
Word on our hearts, but one day we shall know even as we
are known (by God,) and we shall see 'face to face' (1
Corinthians 13:12).

This context for true believers contrasts dramatically with
the horror of that last day for those who do not have the Spirit
and who have tried to lead God's people astray. Their experience of eternity is altogether different, for their condemnation is certain and has already been described (verse 4).

The application of this command and its context is again something the church of all ages must examine. The response of love for God through obedience to his law is all too easily ignored. 'Obedience' is not something that sits well in modern society and this has affected many Christians who see no need to be seen to be different from those around. They emphasise their love for God in romantic terms of good feelings and yet ignore that their love is to be seen, as Jesus himself put it, in obedience and living the sort of life God demands. This is not easy, for we live in the last times, but we look forward to the time when we will be confirmed in righteousness for ever, and meanwhile we press on with the Spirit's help to live obedient lives thus keeping ourselves in the love of God.

Jude now moves on (verses 22-23). The faithful believers in the church not only have to protect themselves but they also need to know how to deal with those around them who may be influenced by the godless men. Although the Greek is not as clear as we might wish at this point, it does seem that Jude here provides us with another threesome. There are three categories of people who will each need to be dealt with in a slightly different way: those who, under the influence of the false teachers, have doubts; those who, being weak spiritually, are in danger of being burned by the sin around them; those who could be genuinely dangerous to the faithful.

b) Do what you can for these godless people (verses 22-23)
First, Jude talks of those who have doubts. Using his fifth command he says, **Be merciful to those who doubt**. It is probably the case that at some time in their lives all Christians have doubts about their faith, but usually these are fleeting and at such times we remind ourselves that our faith is dependent on God and his promises rather than on our feelings or our intellectual prowess. However, some doubting is more

fundamental than this and is often caused by teachers who
raise questions and seek to lead in a different direction. We
have seen how the 'godless' men, 'without the Spirit', have
denied God's grace and led people away from God's word.
This has caused some in the congregation to have real doubts
and questions. Who is right? Are they right to continue in the
teachings they received when they first became Christians or
is it better to follow what they are now hearing, specially as
it seems so persuasive and these people seem so charming?

Almost any minister in any church today will agree that
this problem faces their congregations again and again. Often
nowadays those doubts are sown by people reading books
that lead astray, but sometimes doubts are stirred up by others
in a congregation who will not follow the Lord and his Word
and who pour scorn on the faithful preaching of that Word.
Some begin to doubt when they hear people saying it is un-
intellectual or naive to believe Scripture, or when they see a
leader not living according to what is being preached.
Whatever the cause of these doubts, the problem is ever with
the church.

Jude's advice needs to be heeded. 'Be merciful.' It is all
too easy to make hasty judgments on such people, to criticise
them too strongly and even to separate from them. To do this
may have the opposite of what should be desired. Just as in
verse 21 Christians were reminded that they await the day of
God's final demonstration of mercy to them, so they too need
to show mercy, as they seek to restore these people, answer
their questions, and their doubts and lead them back to the
true path of God's way for their lives.

The second group Jude knows will be encountered leads
to his sixth command: **snatch others from the fire and save
them**. This group of people are those who are in real and
imminent danger of being burned by sin. In Amos 4:11, we
have a picture of God snatching Israel from the fire: '"You

were like a burning stick snatched from the fire, yet you have not returned to me," declares the LORD.' Zechariah also provides an interesting background in the passage where the high priest Joshua is standing before the angel of the LORD with Satan ready to accuse him. The Lord then defends Joshua by saying, 'Is not this man a burning stick snatched from the fire?' (3:2).

The Greek of verse 23 makes the word 'save' the command ('but save some through snatching them from the fire'). Salvation belongs to the Lord. The Christian's job, however, is to ensure this salvation is proclaimed to people, specially here to those who, having a weak faith, have moved into areas of serious danger. The task is to draw them back quickly. 'Snatching' carries that sense of urgency Jude wants us to hear. We will do this by pointing back to Christ and his mercy, to his Word and to the 'faith once and for all entrusted to the saints' (verse 3).

Just as a father might snatch his child out of the path of a bus, so it is our duty to watch over each other and pull back those who, through weakness of faith or understanding, are finding themselves drawn towards the fire. Involvement with sin will burn and destroy. In this sense at least there is not a shadow of doubt that we are indeed 'our brother's keeper'! We need to be concerned for each other as Christians, constantly exhorting and helping each other to contend for the faith and remain steadfast in the love of God.

The third group Jude is concerned for are those who have moved far enough under the influence of the godless leaders that they are actually becoming dangerous to the faithful. This gives rise to a repetition of Jude's fifth command: **to others, show mercy, mixed with fear – hating even the clothing stained by corrupted flesh**. Still Jude wants those who are contending for the faith to be merciful just as Christ is merciful to them. However, being merciful and seeking to draw people back into the way of truth does not mean that there is no danger. When dealing with those who have become involved with the teachings of 'these men', when dealing with those who are already involved in their immorality and godlessness, there is a real danger that the faithful might also be tempted to stray. The attractions of sin must never be underestimated. Too often people feel that somehow they are immune to certain temptations of the flesh, but such feelings often result in downfall as they succumb to sin themselves. So Jude gives sensible advice to the faithful.

By all means, do not separate yourself entirely from such people. Do not run away and set up another church. Do not expel such people from your house-group, but be prepared to forgive and welcome back: have mercy. In doing this, though, also have a healthy fear. There is a very important balance here. To show mercy is not the same thing as fully accepting someone whose sin might well lead others astray. Having mercy is to spend time with that person pointing out their sin and the forgiveness of God that awaits the repentant sinner, but it is not to be gullible.

There is far too little fear these days of those in our midst who are entrenched in sinful ways, and persist in their sin. Too often Christians are tempted to say, 'Well, that is just the way so and so is! I don't think we can do anything about it!' The gullible acceptance of continuing sin in a church simply because we heed the call to have mercy is to be unbalanced and naive. Jude wants us to be truly fearful for ourselves even as we reach out to others. If I see someone about to fall over a cliff, I will rush forward to try and pull the person back, but I would surely seek in every possible way to avoid going over the cliff myself. So with Christians who seem to have got caught up in the ways of falsehood and sin, the church needs to continue to show mercy but with a real fear lest others too should be drawn off track.

Jude emphasises this with his next comment – **hating even the clothing stained by corrupted flesh**. The picture is strong. The word for clothing refers to undergarments and the idea is that just as Jude's readers would steer clear of someone else's dirty and 'stained' undergarments, so they should stay far away from the sinful ways this group may be following. In the same way as one might fear contamination and illness from touching someone else's clothing stained by bodily discharge, so one should fear the contamination of sin. The emphasis on undergarments probably specially recalls the sin of immorality with which the false teachers are so closely associated. But the principle is universally true for the believer. Hatred of sinful activity should be second nature to the one who has been 'born from above' and is now a 'new creation in Christ'.

This is not so much a call to separate the sin from the sinner (for sin only exists as the sinner commits the sin), but rather a call to deal with the person as one needing forgiveness and mercy, yet one from whom we must keep a healthy distance lest we too become contaminated with the same sin.

Again Jude pleads for a sensible balance as the Christian and the church confront sinful people who need forgiveness. Showing love and mercy should not lead to involvement in their pagan life-style. A Christian does not need to commit adultery to be able to minister to an adulterer with mercy and with love. The church does not have to examine pornography in order to take a person caught up with pornography and show love and point to God's mercy and forgiveness. These distinctions are so often forgotten in the modern church. Seeking to become involved with society in order to reach sinners with God's mercy, the church has often become corrupted and no longer able to see sin for what it is – something of which we should be deeply fearful.

7. Glory to the Only God (verses 24-25)

Jude has finished his exhortation to the faithful. He has finished warning against the ungodly and deceitful people who have slipped into the church, and now he focuses the reader's thinking once again on the God of all grace with whom he started his epistle.

In these two verses, Jude uses the form of a doxology, a hymn or statement which brings glory to God, to commend these Christians to the mercy and grace of God who alone can ultimately protect them and preserve them.

a) God will protect you (verse 24)

To him who is able to keep you from falling and to present you before his glorious presence without fault and with great joy ... be glory.

Jude has in mind the final day when Christians stand before their Maker. It is common to talk of 'standing' or 'falling' when coming before God. On that judgment day it will be only justified sinners who will 'stand'. They are the ones who have been declared 'not guilty' in advance on the basis of the saving death of Christ on the cross. They will be without fault on that day. This saving grace is appropriated through faith but comes entirely of God's grace and so it is fully appropriate as Jude ends this letter that he should commend his people to the God who alone **is able to keep** them **from falling and to present** them (to make them stand) in his **glorious presence**. The 'presence of his glory' (Greek) refers to the revelation of God himself that will take place on that occasion.

Is it any wonder that they will be full of joy on that day? Jude has held the fear of this judgment day over the heads of those who are godless and devoid of the Holy Spirit, but for those who belong to Christ, who have the Spirit, who are justified by faith, there is no fear of that day for it will be a time of glorious joy – the fulfilment of all that has been awaited through the entire length of 'the last times' when things have been far from easy (verse 18).

Although the Greek word for **falling** is rare and really means 'stumbling', the sense is obvious and again recalls other passages of both the Old and New Testaments. For example, in Psalm 121:3-8 we read: 'The LORD will not let your foot slip – he who watches over you will not slumber ... the LORD will keep you from all harm ... both now and for evermore.' The apostle Paul appeals to this keeping power of God in 1 Corinthians 1:8, 'He will keep you strong to the end, so that you will be blameless on the day of our Lord Jesus Christ.'[20] This doctrine, that is sometimes called the 'perseverance of the saints' is one of the most wonderful in Scripture as we saw when we looked at verse 1. It is entirely appropriate that Jude should return to it as he ends an epistle that has warned against those who would lead God's people astray. To know that God is the Saviour who 'began a good work' in us and 'will carry it on to completion until the day of Christ Jesus' (Philippians 1:6) is the truth that brings all Christians through the ages great comfort and assurance.

b) Glory to God (verse 25)
Verse 25 then continues praise to this wonderful Saviour God: **to the only God our Saviour be glory, majesty, power and authority, through Jesus Christ our Lord, before all ages, now and for evermore! Amen**.

As the epistle comes to an end, it is possible to imagine the whole congregation shouting 'Amen' with Jude. God's kingly glory is specially emphasised here with reference to his majesty, power and authority. He is the King with ultimate power and authority for he is the **only God**. But that glory

---

20. See also 1 Thessalonians 5:23 and 2 Thessalonians 3:3.

and majesty and power and authority is mediated to us through Jesus Christ our Lord. Thus as we ascribe glory to God we do so remembering that in Christ we have come to know that glory and authority and power. Indeed through Christ we have come to know how God is indeed the Saviour.

It is not at all surprising that these last two verses have become one of the most popular benedictions used these days at the end of worship services. They do for us what they did for Jude. They summarise the continuing sovereign work of God through Jesus on our behalf, and ascribe to him all the glory.

Nothing is beyond God's majestic and sovereign control. It is he who keeps his people from falling and it is to him that individual Christians and the church at large are to bring their whole selves as an offering of thanksgiving to him.

Final thoughts
Jude has written to a church suffering from severe problems with godless leaders who think they are spiritual yet in reality do not have the Spirit. Their doom has been prophesied and the Old Testament provides ample examples of what happens to those who continue to scoff at God's Word, to grumble at his commands, and to lead others astray. For those who remain faithful, there is the reminder that God has called them, loved them and will keep them for that last day when, unlike the false leaders, they will be found to be without fault and will be presented before God, faultless. No wonder Jude says they will be full of joy on that staggering occasion when Christ returns. Though these 'last times' will be full of difficulties and temptations, yet the faithful should build themselves up on the most holy faith and contend for it. They should be a praying people, helped by the Holy Spirit to live a life of love for God shown through obedience to him. But in the end the full credit for their salvation goes entirely **to the only God our Saviour**.

Prayer: O God who art the author of peace and lover of concord, in knowledge of whom standeth our eternal life, whose service is perfect freedom, defend us thy humble servants in all assaults of our enemies, that we, surely trusting in thy defence, may not fear the power of any adversaries, through the might of Jesus Christ our Lord. Amen.

Appendix on Jude's use of the Book of Enoch

Jude mentions this work, known to us as 1 Enoch, in verses 14-15. However, some themes found in Enoch are to be found elsewhere in Jude as well. For example, the theme of 'ungodliness' and the 'ungodly' figures prominently in Enoch. Jude's idea of 'denial' (they 'deny Jesus Christ our only Sovereign and Lord', Jude 4) is reminiscent of Enoch's talk of those who are 'denying the Lord of the Spirits' (1 Enoch 38:2; 41:2; etc.)

However, it is clear that Enoch is a pseudonymous book. In other words it was not written by Enoch himself whose life is mentioned in Genesis 5:19-24. Indeed this pseudonymity is one of the several reasons why the book was never accepted as part of the canon of Scripture either in the Jewish synagogue or in the Christian church. The work was well respected, though, specially in the days in which Jude was writing, perhaps much as we might respect a good commentary on the Bible. In other words, it was regarded as a reliable exposition of the events it described.

Our problem is that Jude quotes Enoch as 'prophecy' (verse 14) to make his point in his own *canonical* book of Scripture. Does this mean that he thereby gives 1 Enoch an equivalent status with *Scripture*? One or two early church leaders and

writers believed that it did. Others have suggested that Jude
is saying no more than that particular statements in the book
of Enoch were inspired, namely those repeated by Jude. But
is it necessary even to say this much? We should note that
Jude does not refer to this writing as 'Scripture', nor does he
begin the quotation with the normal New Testament clause:
'it is written...' This is at least one indication that Jude did
not regard the work as inspired or part of the canon.
Nevertheless, his readers may well have given it a rather
superior status.

It is possible that Jude did believe that the true Enoch really
prophesied judgment.[21] We have no record of any such
prophecy in Scripture, but the information we do have about
Enoch may point to the fact that he might have been regarded
as a prophet from earliest times. In Genesis 5:22 Methuselah
was born to Enoch. Enoch is described as 'righteous' and as
'walking with God' before 'God took him away'. It was just
as Methuselah died that the flood came, so perhaps in giving
his son the name Methuselah, Enoch may have had a prophetic
insight about the coming judgment. But we cannot be sure of
any of this and perhaps it is best to see 1 Enoch as a book that
Jude was prepared to use whenever it accurately interpreted
or applied *biblical* truth.

He did this, it seems, because his *readers* regarded it so
highly. He therefore was, in effect, using their own material
to point to their own judgment. A paraphrase of Jude's

21. Or perhaps Jude may have thought that the section he quoted was a
genuine prophecy of Enoch. It has been suggested that someone might have
had a dream or revelation indicating that this part of Enoch did originate
from the time before the flood. But all such ideas are simply speculation
and we need to be careful not to defend Jude with suggestions for which we
have no basis. As seen in this Appendix, Jude does not need defending in
this way. Rather we should understand that Jude is simply using Enoch as a
source for a prophecy often repeated in the pages of the canon – a prophecy
that God will come to this earth to judge the ungodly.

intention might go something like this: 'Here is a book you know well; it contains much that is useful. We can learn a number of things from it. In some places we can learn from its interpretation of parts of the Old Testament; you need specially to hear these words for they relate to you!'

In citing Enoch, Jude thereby gives the book itself no more authority than we might give, say, to Calvin, when we recognise that on a particular verse, and under the Spirit's guidance, he has opened up the canonical Word to us. The use of a quote from Calvin becomes even more effective if we are speaking to people who regard him highly!

Background to the Book of Enoch

In Jewish intertestamental times there was a great emphasis on the activity of angels and on the final judgment of the wicked and the coming of the Messiah. These great themes, all of which have their roots in the Bible, were developed, understandably, against a background of the Jewish people having returned from captivity in Babylon and having rebuilt the temple and yet still finding themselves a people under the rule of another empire. Where was God in all this? Traditions, theories and explanations of all sorts abounded. 1 Enoch was part of all this and Jude was writing to a readership caught up with such ideas. In quoting this work, Jude was therefore adding weight to *his* argument, for he had found truth *in the passage quoted* from the book of Enoch.

In conclusion, we need to defend Jude for using an apocryphal book anymore than we need to defend the apostle Paul for referring to Cleanthes (2 Timothy 3:8) or Menander (1 Corinthians 15:33). In terms of the inspiration or otherwise of the words quoted, *in their context within Jude* they are inspired by the Holy Spirit and carry the same authority therefore as any other Scripture. That does not mean, though, that all of 1 Enoch or Menander's poetry etc. are to be regarded

as inspired by God's Holy Spirit *outside* the context of Holy
Scripture. The words are inspired by virtue of Jude's use of
the ideas and words because he is an author of canonical
Scripture and was himself thus directed by the Holy Spirit.

STUDY GUIDE

Those using this study guide should first read the appropriate section in the Bible and think about it for themselves. Then they should read what the author says about that section in his commentary. Every question is based on what the author says.

STUDY QUESTIONS ON 2 PETER

1. Greetings from Simon Peter (2 Peter 1:1-2)
1. Who wrote this letter?
2. What does verse 1 tell us about the author?
3. Explain what is precious about our faith. What is faith?
4. What is offered through the knowledge of God and of Jesus our Lord?
5. Describe what is special about being an apostle.
6. The 'righteousness of our God' refers to which two things?
7. What does it mean to enter into the 'covenant relationship with God'?
8. How can we receive 'knowledge of God'?

2. Peter's gospel (2 Peter 1:3-11)
1. What are some of God's 'very great and precious promises'?
2. How can we escape the corruption in the world caused by evil?
3. What are the qualities of a godly life?
4. Would your family detect these qualities in your life?
5. What is the reward if you do these things?
6. How are we shown God's glory?
7. How are we to respond to God's grace and love?
8. What is shown by failing to grow in Christ?

3. Remembering this gospel (2 Peter 1. 12-21)
1. Peter is aware that soon he will die. What emphasis does he put on this life?
2. Summarise 'these things' spoken of in verses 12 and 15.
3. Describe the benefits of remembering the gospel.
4. What were the disciples taught through the transfiguration?
5. Why is the transfiguration evidence of the second coming of Christ?

6. What other evidence in 2 Peter 1:12-21 is there which points to the second coming?
7. Discuss the questions asked on page 52:
    a) To what extent do we live in the light of the truth?
    b) To what extent do we let it govern our lives?

4. Beware of false prophets (2 Peter 2:1-10a)
1. Why are we to be wary of false teachers?
2. What do the flood and the destruction of Sodom and Gomorrah in verses 4-9 teach us about God's judgement?
3. How do we recognise false prophets?
4. This section warns us of God's destruction on those who teach heresies. Discuss what we learn from this
        a) individually
        b) as a church
5. From 2 Peter 2:1, who brings swift destruction on themselves and how?
6. What made Lot and Noah righteous?
7. Consider ways in which we can preach righteousness.
8. Compare the people Lot and Noah faced with the people we face today.

5. Recognise false prophets and teachers (2 Peter 2:10b-22)
1. Compare 'brute beasts' to false teachers and prophets.
2. Are we becoming too tolerant of evil?
3. God is a just God. How dose he deal with those who
        a) act like animals.
        b) harm others.
        c) blaspheme and slander.
4. How were the false teachers like Baalam?
5. Why is it important to have good teachers in the church?
6. How do we find true freedom?
7. What are the signs in a person's life that show he is a Christian?

6. Remember – Christ will return (2 Peter 3:1-18)
1. From verses 1 and 2, what did Peter want the readers to remember?
2. How should we react to scoffing about the second coming?
3. By forgetting the creating word of God, what else were they trying to hide?

4. How should we live, knowing that Christ will return?
5. What principles should guide us when we talk of God?
6. Although God is not bound by time, how does scripture reveal God to us in terms of linear time?
7. What does it mean to live holy and godly lives?
8. Why can Christians never fear the coming of Christ?
9. What three things explain the fullness of what God is saying to us?

7. Closing remarks (2 Peter 3:17-18)
1. How can we be on our guard?
2. What is 'your secure position'?
3. How can you grow in grace and knowledge of our Lord?
4. How do we give glory to the Lord?
5. What will the resurrected body be like?

JUDE
1. Greetings from Jude (1-2)
1. How does Jude describe himself?
2. Who is he writing to?
3. Who is called and how?
4. How was the love of God most clearly shown?
5. What is offered in verse 2?

2. Jude's reason for writing (3-4)
1. As Christians, what do we all have in common?
2. What is salvation?
3. What is faith?
4. What was Jude's original topic? What did he write about instead?
5. Think about the harm that could be caused by 'godless men' who 'have secretly slipped in among you'.
6. Explain what it means to be godless.
7. What is the mark of belonging to Christ?
8. How should this encourage us to live?

3. Good grounds for urgency (5-7)
1. From these verse what do we find the Scriptures useful for?
2. From part (a), what can we learn from the past?
3. How did the angels fall?

4. What awaits those fallen angels and therefore false teachers on the Day of Judgement?
5. What does Jude want the people to learn from Sodom and Gomorrah?
6. What common end do the three references to sexual immorality have?
7. What two pressures must we flee from?
8. Are you becoming more accepting of immorality in the world around you?

4. These godless people also face judgement (8-13)
1. When people speak of having had a dream in which God has spoken to them, what should we be careful of?
2. What are the three points of comparison that Jude makes to 'these men'?
3. What can we learn from the archangel Michael?
4. What does verse 10 show us about these men's understanding?
5. What did Cain, Baalam and Korah have in common?
6. Cain lacked faith. What did that lead to?
7. What is the messsage Jude ultimately wants us to get from verse 11?
8. When writing of autumn leaves, Jude calls them twice dead. What comparison does this make with the ungodly leaders?

5. Their judgement was predicted (14-19)
1. Who will be the judge in the last days?
2. What are the characteristics of the ungodly?
3. Consider each sin and how easily they slip into our churches today – grumbling, fault-finding, evil desires, boasting and flattery.
4. How can our churches become stronger?
5. Are we ready for Christ's return?
6. How do godly leaders seek to bring unity to the church?
7. Some argue that homosexual relations exist due to genetics. What response should we make if faced with this issue?

6. Jude's summary and appeal for urgent precautions (20-23)
1. What does 'your most holy faith' mean?
2. What is a healthy church committed to?
3. How do we build ourselves up?
4. How does the Holy Spirit help us to pray?

5. How important is the prayer meeting in your church?
6. How should we live from day to day as God's people?
7. In what ways can we help people with doubts about their faith?
8. How can we 'snatch others from the fire and save them'?
9. 'The church has often become corrupted and no longer able to see sin for what it is' (p. 227). How should we as the church try to avoid this?

7. Glory to the Only God (24-25)
1. What day does Jude refer to here?
2. What truth brings all Christians comfort and assurance?
3. How do we know that God is the Saviour?

Christian Focus Publications publishes biblically-accurate books for adults and children. The books in the adult range are published in three imprints.

Christian Heritage contains classic writings from the past.

Christian Focus contains popular works including biographies, commentaries, doctrine, and Christian living.

Mentor focuses on books written at a level suitable for Bible College and seminary students, pastors, and others; the imprint includes commentaries, doctrinal studies, examination of current issues, and church history.

For a free catalogue of all our titles, please write to
Christian Focus Publications,
Geanies House, Fearn,
Ross-shire, IV20 1TW, Great Britain

For details of our titles visit us on our web site
http://www.christianfocus.com